IMAGES OF WAR

THE WAR IN THE SOUTH PACIFIC

RARE PHOTOGRAPHS FROM WARTIME ARCHIVES

Jon Diamond

Pen & Sword
MILITARY

First published in Great Britain in 2017 by
PEN & SWORD MILITARY
An imprint of
Pen & Sword Books Ltd
47 Church Street
Barnsley
South Yorkshire
S70 2AS

ISBN 978-1-47387-061-1

Typeset by Concept, Huddersfield, West Yorkshire HD4 5JL.
Printed and bound in Great Britain by
CPI Group (UK) Ltd, Croydon, CR0 4YY

Pen & Sword Books Ltd incorporates the imprints of Pen & Sword Archaeology, Atlas, Aviation, Battleground, Discovery, Family History, History, Maritime, Military, Naval, Politics, Railways, Select, Social History, Transport, True Crime, and Claymore Press, Frontline Books, Leo Cooper, Praetorian Press, Remember When, Seaforth Publishing and Wharncliffe.

For a complete list of Pen & Sword titles please contact
PEN & SWORD BOOKS LIMITED
47 Church Street, Barnsley, South Yorkshire S70 2AS, England
E-mail: enquiries@pen-and-sword.co.uk
Website: www.pen-and-sword.co.uk

Contents

About the Author

Jon Diamond is an American practising physician in Pennsylvania. He graduated from Cornell University and was on the faculties of Harvard Medical School and the Pennsylvania State University College of Medicine, achieving the academic rank of Professor at the latter. A lifelong student of military history, Jon has contributed numerous articles to Sovereign Media's *WWII History*, *WWII Quarterly*, *Military History*, and *Civil War Quarterly*. He was a civilian attendee at the National Security Seminar at the United States Army War College in Carlisle, Pennsylvania. He has authored four Osprey Publishing books and three Stackpole Military Photo Series volumes. His Pen & Sword *Images of War* Series works include: *Stilwell and the Chindits: The Allied Campaign in Northern Burma 1943–1944* and *The Fall of Malaya and Singapore*. Currently, he is working on his latest *Images of War* Series book, *The Invasion of Sicily 1943*. As a physician, Jon takes care of many Second World War veterans, who are becoming a dwindling cadre due to the inexorable march of time. We listen to their accounts and read about their exploits lest we forget their sacrifice to preserve freedom.

Acknowledgements

The Author wishes to thank the Archivists at the United States Army Military Heritage Institute (USAMHI), Carlisle Barracks, Carlisle, Pennsylvania and the Still Photo Section, National Archives and Records Administration (NARA), College Park, Maryland for their assistance in locating the many photographic files used in the preparation of this book. The author also wishes to acknowledge the cartographic expertise of Phillip Schwartzberg of Meridian Mapping in Minneapolis, Minnesota for his helpful suggestions about map composition. This book is dedicated to all of the men and women who served during the epic struggle up the Solomon Island chain from 1942–1945.

Chapter One

Overview of the South Pacific Campaign

Key Allied victories in the Pacific have been singled out as seminal turning points against the Japanese. The American Navy's sinking of four enemy carriers at Midway crippled future Imperial Japanese Navy (IJN) initiatives on the scale mounted during the war's initial six months. The six-month gruelling defence and ultimate conquest of Guadalcanal by American land, sea and air forces, after the initial Marine amphibious invasion of that Southern Solomon Island on 7 August 1942, halted the Japanese south-eastward strategic advance to sever the sea lanes to the Antipodes. What has become ignored, however, is the back-breaking series of defeats that the Japanese suffered in their attempts to defend the New Georgia group of islands and Bougainville in the Central and Northern Solomon Islands respectively. The toll in Imperial Japanese Army (IJA) units, naval ships, aircraft and crews could never be replaced by the Japanese after the defeats suffered on these hellacious jungle islands, especially given the requisite presence of Imperial forces on other fronts, including the Central Pacific, New Guinea and the Asian mainland.

By the first week of February 1943, the Guadalcanal campaign was won by the US Marines, Army and Navy after almost six horrific months of jungle combat, aerial attacks and naval surface action. However, the Japanese did not consider Guadalcanal's evacuation to be more than a temporary setback in the South Pacific. Both the emperor and the imperial general staff commented that the Japanese forces were simply changing emphasis. For several months they had been on the offensive in the Solomon Islands area and on the defensive in Papua, New Guinea. A reversal was to occur. As for the IJA, the important matter was the capture of all of New Guinea, with a renewed drive for Port Moresby out of Lae near the Huon Gulf of North-east New Guinea. The Solomon Islands in the South Pacific sector were to be primarily an IJN problem. This disunity in effort and planning was to plague the Japanese Armed Forces in subsequent campaigns after their lightning string of victories from December 1941 to June 1942.

The head of the Japanese Combined Fleet, Admiral Isoruku Yamamoto, sorely wanted to regain the strategic initiative and, perhaps, win one additional major victory

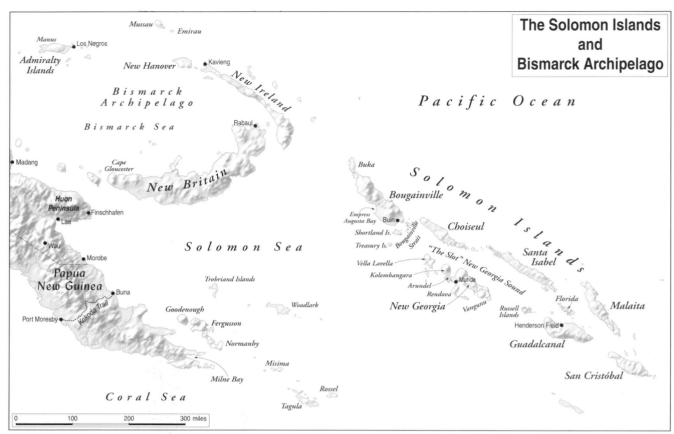

Map 1. The South Pacific Area, comprising the Solomon Islands, under the command of Vice Admiral William F. Halsey, and the South-west Pacific Area, principally New Guinea, the Bismarck Archipelago and surrounding island groups, under the leadership of General Douglas A. MacArthur are shown. Both American commanders, along with their Allied forces, were to conduct separate amphibious and land campaigns to retake the Solomon Islands, New Guinea and adjacent sites, such as Cape Gloucester on New Britain, from the Japanese. As more proximate air-bases to Rabaul were acquired or constructed, such as on Bougainville, an intensified air interdiction campaign to neutralize that Japanese bastion on New Britain, Operation *Cartwheel*, would be conducted by Allied air assets stationed in both theatres, such that a bloody and protracted amphibious operation against that enemy fortified base could be avoided. After Guadalcanal, the unoccupied Russell Islands in the Southern Solomons were taken on 21 February by Halsey's South Pacific Force. IJN Admiral Isoroku Yamamoto had drawn a line through the Central Solomons as the new Japanese defensive Front. In July 1943, Halsey breached this Japanese defensive line with his amphibious invasion of the New Georgia group, including Rendova, New Georgia, Arundel and Vella Lavella in the Central Solomons. In order to protect MacArthur's eastern flank for his upcoming Cape Gloucester and Arawe landings on the western and southern shores of New Britain by Marine and US Army forces respectively in December 1943, Halsey's South Pacific Force was tasked with the amphibious invasion of Bougainville at Empress Augusta Bay on 1 November 1943. As a result of Halsey and MacArthur's parallel campaigns in their respective theatres, IJN and IJA commanders at Rabaul were limited to making piecemeal ground and air reinforcements to their garrisons in the Solomons and on New Guinea. Given the fact that Rabaul was also under Allied air attack along two axes, a major IJN counter-offensive never materialized, with Imperial surface vessels merely attempting to disrupt Allied amphibious operations.

(*Philip Schwartzberg, Meridian Mapping*)

since the 'invincible years' of 1941–1942. After the evacuation of Guadalcanal, during the initial week of February 1943, Yamamoto drew a new defensive line in the South Pacific through the middle of the Solomons. Yamamoto had moved his advanced IJN bases back to New Georgia and Kolombangara in the Central Solomon Islands. With Guadalcanal's evacuation, Imperial Headquarters in Tokyo made plans to reinforce the area and seize victory again. It was Yamamoto's hopeful anticipation that a much-desired decisive Japanese victory in 1943 may yet compel the Allies to seek a nego-tiated peace and allow the Japanese to keep their new Pacific empire. The IJA and IJN would have to work together with the latter bringing in supplies and reinforcements to the former.

Yamamoto would be responsible for operations in the Solomons, while Lieutenant General Hitoshi Imamura, the 8th Area Army commander on Rabaul, would be responsible for ground forces in the Central and Northern Solomons. These IJN ground forces were to be comprised of the 17th Army under Lieutenant General Harukichi (Seikichi) Hyakutake in the Solomon Islands, while in Eastern New Guinea the 18th Army, under Lieutenant General Hatazo Adachi, would oversee operations. On Bougainville in the Northern Solomons, the IJN 6th Division would be stationed under 8th Area Army control. Ironically, during a morale-boosting trip to the Northern Solomons on 18 April, Yamamoto's personal IJN twin-engined, land-based Mitsubishi G4M3 'Betty' bomber was shot down over the southern tip of Bougainville by American P-38 fighters stationed on Guadalcanal as the admiral was in flight to Ballale airfield, on a nearby islet in Bougainville Strait. Admiral Mineichi Kogo took over the Combined Fleet after Yamamoto's death.

After Guadalcanal, the Japanese still retained a distinct advantage in the Solomons, even though they had lost the ferociously contested Southern Solomon Island. Their fighter aircraft, the IJN A6M Reisen or 'Zero', along with the IJA Ki-43 Hayabusa or 'Oscar', had longer ranges (approaching 2,000 miles) than the American planes. Additionally, Yamamoto had been continually building up his above-mentioned air-fields in the Northern Solomons as staging areas as well as at Vila on Kolombangara and at Munda on New Georgia. Japanese planes could, thus, be dispatched from Rabaul to New Georgia, where they could refuel, go on to attack the American bases at Tulagi and Guadalcanal, and then return the same way with many emergency airfields, if needed, to conserve the diminishing number of skilled pilots, many of whom had been lost in air combat over Guadalcanal and Papua, New Guinea. The American planes, especially the fighters, did not have the range to reach Rabaul and return to US bases. Recognizing this logistical advantage, Yamamoto was going to reinvigorate his air attacks on Guadalcanal from his bases on Rabaul after the Japanese evacuation from that bitterly contested island in early February 1943.

The Solomon Island chain, consisting of six major islands and many smaller ones, is over 500 miles in length. Bougainville is one of the most northern in the island chain as well as the largest, being 130 miles in length and 30 miles in width. Bougainville is located 300 miles to north of Guadalcanal. Also to the north of Guadalcanal lie the islands in the Central Solomons, with the largest Japanese base there at Munda on New Georgia. Other islands in the area include Kolombangara, Arundel, Rendova, Vella Lavella, Ganongga, Tetipari, Gatukai, Vangunu and many smaller islands. The island of New Georgia refers to the largest one in the group of eleven main Central Solomon Islands. The approximate centre of the Central Solomon group is at Munda Point on the south-west tip of New Georgia island, about 170 miles west north-west of Tulagi and Guadalcanal, with the small group known as the Russell Islands some 125 miles to the south-east serving as the obvious stepping-stone between New Georgia and Guadalcanal. Rendova Island is located about 7 miles to the south of New Georgia across the Blanche Channel. The proximity of Rendova to Munda Point would play a major role in Vice-Admiral William F. 'Bull' Halsey's strategic plans for his offensive after securing the Russell Islands following the American victory on Guadalcanal.

New Georgia is 45 by 35 miles and suitable landing beaches were few in number. Immediately inland from the coast were rugged, jungle-covered cliffs. The terrain of New Georgia was typical for the islands in the Central Solomons, being rugged with heavy rain forest covering volcanic cores. The Japanese reconnoitred New Georgia in October 1942, with the intent to build suitable airfields to support the action on Guadalcanal. As early as December 1942, American scout planes discovered the Japanese hard at work on a well-camouflaged airfield at Munda Point on New Georgia. Elements of the Sasebo 6th Special Naval Landing Force (SNLF), along with some IJA detachments and construction crews, had arrived in late November. American pilots also observed that another Japanese airfield was being completed at Vila Point on Kolombangara, across the Kula Gulf from north-western New Georgia. In early February 1943, the Japanese evacuated Guadalcanal for their new base on New Georgia.

Between February and May 1943, the Japanese reinforced New Georgia with additional IJA and SNLF troops, guessing correctly that this would be one of Halsey's upcoming objectives. The Japanese command had incorrectly concluded that Kolombangara, north of Munda Airfield, would be assaulted by the Allies first, prior to a landing on New Georgia. All Japanese forces defending Kolombangara and New Georgia were placed under the command of Major General Noboru Sasaki of the 38th Infantry Group, comprised of elements of the IJA 6th and 38th Divisions, with headquarters at Vila and designated as South-east Detachment under the administrative direction of IJA 17th Army and IJN 8th Fleet situated at Rabaul. By the time of Halsey's invasion in July 1943, there would be 5,000 IJA and 5,500 SNLF troops on New Georgia, with an additional 4,200 troops from both forces on Santa Isabel

Island, located to the north-east of New Georgia and directly north of the Russell Islands and the north-western tip of Guadalcanal.

Topographically, Bougainville possesses two central mountain ranges – the Emperor Range in the north, and the lower, less-rugged one to the south, the Crown Prince Range. The former has two active volcanoes, Mount Balbi, at over 10,000 feet and Mount Bagana. Except for some roads in the south that could accommodate wheeled transport, overland movement was limited to primitive trails through the dense jungle interior. Most important of the island routes was the Numa Numa Trail, which extended south-west from Numa Numa on the north-east coast to Empress Augusta Bay, and the East–West Trail, running north-west from Buin on the southern tip to Gazelle Harbor below Empress Augusta Bay.

Bougainville's strategic importance rested on its location, being just over 200 air miles from Rabaul. The Japanese bastion of Rabaul, directly to the north-west of Bougainville, was the headquarters and main supply base for both the Japanese South-eastern Army and the South-eastern Fleet. Rabaul is situated at the extreme north-east tip of New Britain, in the Bismarck Archipelago on the shore of Simpson Harbor, which is roughly 400 miles from Port Moresby in Papua and 600 miles from Guadalcanal. This excellent location gave the Japanese the ability to dominate northern New Guinea, the Bismarck Archipelago and the Solomon Islands chain. Air units based at Rabaul were the responsibility of the Eleventh Air Fleet. Despite extensive losses, the IJN continued to reinforce its air units with approximately fifty planes a month flown in from Truk in the Caroline Islands. By May 1942, Rabaul, in the South Pacific, had replaced Truk, in the Central Pacific's Caroline Islands, as the Japanese citadel in the Pacific.

In all of New Britain, the IJA could muster over 97,000 men. To defend the region around Rabaul in November 1943, the IJA had over 76,000 men. There were four natural harbours there, with Simpson Harbor capable of handling 300,000 tons of shipping with its excellent docking facilities. As Admiral Morison commented, 'Tarawa, Iwo Jima and Okinawa would have faded to pale pink in comparison with the blood that would have flowed if the Allies had attempted an [amphibious] assault on Fortress Rabaul.'

The invasion of Bougainville, along with construction of airfields there, would be a major part in the Allied plan, Operation *Cartwheel*, to completely isolate Rabaul. Bougainville was to be assaulted as the final phase of the bloody campaign up the Solomon Island chain. However, due to Bougainville's proximity to Rabaul, it was heavily garrisoned by the Japanese. Bougainville was headquarters for the Japanese Northern Solomons Defence Force, with its main base of Buin located on the south-eastern tip of the island, across from which were the Shortland Islands, Faisi and Ballale. The IJA 17th Army Headquarters and the IJA 6th Division, the latter having achieved notoriety for atrocities committed in China, had 15,000 men around Buin airfield on the island's southern tip. There were other airfields in the south, including Kahili, Kieta, Tenekau and Kara. The IJN's Eighth Fleet had several hundred more men on Bougainville and there were over 10,000 to 20,000 Japanese troops and naval coast artillery in the Shortland Islands and nearby Ballale Island, the latter with its airfield being entirely an IJN operation. In the extreme north-west of the island, abutting Buka Passage, was an airfield at Bonis. Additionally, at the Buka Island air-base, just to the north of Bougainville, the IJA had garrisoned 5,000 men while the navy stationed 1,000 sailors, the latter at a seaplane base. Intriguingly, at Empress Augusta Bay on the island's western side, which would ultimately be selected as Halsey's amphibious assault target in November 1943, the IJA had stationed only a small infantry garrison.

Operation *Cartwheel*, the Allied plan to neutralize Rabaul by air assault in 1943, after capturing the Solomon Islands from the enemy for their airfields or construction of new ones, was just one of three Allied axes of advance in the Pacific theatre that would reverse the tide of war against Japan. Stanley Frankel, the US Army's 37th Infantry Division's historian, wrote about the Japanese counter-offensive against Bougainville's US Army's XIVth Corps perimeter at Cape Torokina in March 1944:

> The curtain was about to rise on one of the bloodiest, most fanatical *Banzai* attacks made by the Japanese in the South Pacific War ... against a civilian army of battling clerks, farmers, mechanics, schoolboys, businessmen.

Major General Allen H. Turnage, commanding the 3rd Marine Division that had invaded Bougainville in November 1943, said:

> Never had men in the Marine Corps had to fight and maintain themselves over such difficult terrain as was encountered on Bougainville.

Another Marine veteran of Guam and Iwo Jima recounted:

> Of all the twenty-eight months I spent overseas nothing compared to Bougain-ville for miserable living conditions ... Bougainville had to be the closest thing to a living hell that I ever saw in my life.

Lieutenant General Alexander A. Vandegrift, who commanded the 1st Marine Division on Guadalcanal, and then the I Marine Amphibious Corps (IMAC) for the Bougainville landings, commented that the Bougainville 'jungle [was] worse than we had found on Guadalcanal'. But after Guadalcanal, Tarawa, the Marshall Islands, Saipan, Guam, Peleliu, Iwo Jima and Okinawa, to name but a few Pacific island battles that the Marines gallantly assaulted from the sea, the combat on Bougainville by both the Marines and US Army's National Guard Divisions, the 37th and Americal, that relieved them, has been largely forgotten by the aforementioned headline-grabbing amphibious operations.

Possible explanations for the overshadowing of the Solomon Islands campaign, comprising the war in the South Pacific, stems from a paradigm shift in Allied strategy in that theatre. A Japanese intelligence officer, after the war, admitted that after the bloody frontal assaults along Papua's northern coast at Buna during late 1942 into early 1943, the Americans had begun to display a new strategic initiative to invade Japanese-held areas where they were the least heavily defended. He said;

> This was the type of strategy we hated most. The Americans, with minimum losses, attacked and seized a relatively weak area, constructed airfields and then proceeded to cut the supply lines to troops in that area. Without engaging in a large-scale operation, our strongpoints were gradually starved out ... [The] Americans flowed into our weaker points and submerged us, just as water seeks the weakest entry to sink a ship.

Historian Stephen Taafe interprets this emerging strategy as 'cutting off and isolating their strong points and in effect transforming them into vast jungle prison camps'.

On 7 December 1941, the IJN executed Admiral Yamamoto's planned attack at Pearl Harbor on the Hawaiian island of Oahu with six carriers under the direct command of Admiral Chūichi Nagumo. All of the US Navy Pacific Fleet's battleships were hit by torpedo or horizontal bombers. Military installations on shore, such as airfields and army barracks, also suffered grievously. Well over 2,000 sailors, soldiers, airmen and civilians died as a result of the raid. Below, tug boats and salvage crews in ships' launches and whaleboats attempted to put out the raging fires aboard some of the stricken vessels as a search for survivors in the water was also conducted. *(Library of Congress)*

A host of dry-docked naval vessels berthed in the Pearl Harbor Navy Yard, other than battleships, were also struck by Japanese bombs or torpedoes that Sunday morning. Here a destroyer, the USS *Shaw*, becomes a raging inferno after several dive-bombers of the second aerial assault wave attacked. The photograph shows the moment when the forward magazine exploded and the destroyer sunk after the crew was ordered to abandon her. *(Library of Congress)*

Emblematic of Imperial Japan's invincible years of 1941–42, Japanese soldiers celebrate their conquest of American and Filipino forces on the Bataan Peninsula in the Philippines in April 1942. The soldiers raise their hands and *samurai* swords into the air in a *banzai* battle cry, which celebrated a long life for the emperor. *(NARA)*

American prisoners, some with their hands tied behind their back, are allowed only a brief break during the infamous Bataan Death March in April 1942. After a full-scale invasion of Luzon by the Japanese within days of the Pearl Harbor attack, American and Filipino soldiers were forced to retreat into a slim defensive position on the island's western Bataan Peninsula in January 1942. On 9 April 1942, the American and Filipino forces formally surrendered to the Japanese. Immediately thereafter, the Japanese began to march the 12,000 American and 64,000 Filipino prisoners northward on a 60-mile journey into captivity, committing atrocities on the route. The ordeal lasted several days with over 5,000 Americans dying on the way. (*Library of Congress*)

American and Filipino soldiers emerge with their hands raised from the Malinta Tunnel to surrender after a siege by the Japanese on 6 May 1942. The tunnel was a warren of Allied activity, serving as a headquarters, a bomb-proof storage area, along with a 1,000-bed hospital and communication area. This surrender marked the nadir of American combat misfortune in the Pacific and would also herald the Japanese high-water mark of their conquests. (*NARA*)

During their *blitzkrieg* through the
Philippines, Malaya and Singapore, as
well as islands of the South Pacific and
New Guinea, Japanese soldiers quickly
mastered the art of manoeuvre and
fighting in tropical climates. Above, a
heavily camouflaged and kit-laden
Japanese patrol moves across a
swampy creek over an *ad hoc* log
bridge supported on the shoulders of
other soldiers on its way through the
impenetrable Malayan jungle, early
1942. Often outflanking their British,
Indian and Australian foes using the
Malayan jungles, the Japanese
established road-blocks in the enemy's
rear and sowed panic, especially among
the less experienced Indian troops.
(*Author's Collection*)

A Japanese medium tank, with accompanying infantry, moves through the rubble of one of Singapore City's outskirts
in mid-February 1942. Japanese tanks employed by Lieutenant General Tomoyuki Yamashita maximally mounted a
37mm turret gun, which was ill-suited for engaging enemy tanks but capable of knocking out Allied defensive

fortifications. While the IJA
deployed armoured vehicles
against Allied defensive
positions, there were no British
tanks to combat them. Before
the war, British military leaders
on Singapore expressed their
doubts that armour could be
successfully deployed in the
Malayan jungles, and therefore
excluded them from tactical
planning for defence of the
Malayan Peninsula as well as
for Singapore Island. Also,
British Prime Minister Winston
Churchill was more concerned
about sending his available
tanks to North Africa to fight
the Axis and to the Soviet
Union, after June 1941, to
assist his new ally. (*NARA*)

An Argyll and Sutherland Highlander jumps from this Lanchester armoured car in Malaya with a Vickers Mk I medium machine-gun with a front bipod and rear monopod mounted on. The Vickers Mk I gun fired the same .303-inch calibre cartridge as the lighter machine-guns, such as the Bren gun, as well as the standard issue Short Magazine Lee-Enfield (SMLE) rifle. As a result of its water cooling, it was exceptionally suited for continuous firing. The other Highlander to the right readies the water can and ammunition box for the gun. (*Library of Congress*)

Members of the 9th Gurkha Regiment of the Indian Army train with a 3-inch mortar in the Malayan jungle before the Japanese invasion. Along with the British 25-pounder field artillery piece, this weapon was quite effective in disrupting massed Japanese infantry assaults. However, after the Japanese invasion along the eastern Thai coast, the enemy often used the jungle to circumvent Allied defensive positions. (*Library of Congress*)

In the absence of their own armour, an Australian 2-pounder gun-crew fires on a Japanese light tank column at a pre-arranged ambush site on the Muar-Bakri Road in Malaya's Johore Province in the south of the peninsula. Many Japanese light tanks were disabled in this engagement, which was one of the few Allied successes against enemy armour. (NARA)

A camouflaged 15-inch British naval gun emplacement is exhibited on Singapore before hostilities commenced. In the misguided belief that an attack on Singapore would be launched from the sea and not down the Malay Peninsula, two such batteries were present at Buono Vista on the southern coast and the Johore Battery on the island's eastern tip. Although some of the heavy British ordnance could direct fire northwards towards the Japanese 25th Division attacking across the Straits of Johore, the presence of mostly armour-piercing, anti-ship artillery shells proved a detriment for these guns to provide a meaningful component to the defence of Singapore. (Author's Collection)

Native troops from the Straits Settlement Volunteer Forces (SSVF) Brigade line up for an inspection prior to the island's invasion in early February 1942. This unit comprised British, Chinese, Indian and Malay individuals, who fought the Japanese onslaught valiantly. (*Author's Collection*)

Allied infantrymen position themselves along a road in the vicinity of Bukit Timah Hill. A sharp engagement against Japanese tanks and infantry occurred at that site, which only briefly halted the enemy advance. Deficiencies in troop number, communications and heavy armament, much left back on the Malayan Peninsula, contributed to the Japanese overcoming the hastily developed defences at this important site in the centre of Singapore Island near the vital Peirce and MacRitchie Reservoirs. (*Author's Collection*)

Field Marshal Archibald P. Wavell arrives in Batavia, Netherlands East Indies (NEI), for the American-British-Dutch-Australian Command (ABDACOM) Conference in early 1942. This combined ABDACOM structure came into being on 3 January 1942. Wavell established his HQ in Lembang in Java on 15 January 1942 in order to oversee all Allied forces in the Far East. The ABDACOM was disbanded on 22 February 1942, after Hong Kong, Singapore and the NEI had all fallen. (*USAMHI*)

On 15 February 1942, at the Ford Motor Factory near Bukit Timah Hill, British General Officer Commanding, Singapore, Lieutenant General Arthur E. Percival (*second from right*) surrenders to Japanese 25th Army's commander Lieutenant General Tomoyuki Yamashita (*left of Percival*) after the agreement to terms was negotiated. Yamashita negated any delay of formal surrender for fear that Percival's staff would find out how few Japanese troops he had and their almost completely expended lot of artillery ammunition. (*Author's Collection*)

Japanese infantry, with their bayonets fixed to their *Arisaka* rifles, rapidly advance northwards from Rangoon to the outskirts of Mandalay at the end of April 1942. General Sir Harold Alexander had arrived in Burma in early March in an attempt to stem the inexorable Japanese advance, but he was unsuccessful at repeated battle locales. On 26 April, Alexander decided that his main objective was to withdraw as much of his Burma Army as possible to India for reorganization, and to defend the sub-continent from a feared Japanese invasion there. (*Author's Collection*)

A Japanese artillery crew mans its Type 94 (1934) 75mm mountain gun, which most divisional artillery regiments were armed with in Burma during the rapid drive through that Asian mainland country from January to May 1942. To keep up with the tremendous speed of the Japanese infantry against the weakening Allied forces, this gun could be broken down into eleven components for the packhorses to carry. Although antiquated, the quick disassembly of this mountain gun was ideal for the Burmese terrain to support the infantry. (*NARA*)

(**Above**) Indian troops take up defensive positions on the Sittang River, awaiting the Japanese assault. On the night of 22/23 February 1942, an order was given, based on a miscommunication, to blow up the great bridge across the river. The line of retreat of the British and Indian troops still on the eastern side of the river was thus severed. (*NARA*)

(**Opposite above**) Lieutenant General Joseph W. Stilwell leads the 'walkout' from Burma in May 1942. After learning that the Japanese had outstripped his withdrawal towards Myitkyina, Stilwell and a party of 114 British, American and Burmese began their trek both overland and by waterways. They crossed the Chindwin River in dugouts and ferries at Homalin, hours before a Japanese cavalry detachment arrived there. Setting a demanding pace, Stilwell managed to extricate his entire party to safety in India's Assam Province. (*USAMHI*)

(**Opposite below**) Major Michael Calvert of the Royal Engineers (*seated second from right*) is shown at the Bush Warfare School at Maymyo in Burma in early 1942. It was there that Calvert met Orde Wingate, a controversial British officer sent by Wavell into Burma, to conduct behind-the-line commando-type operations to retard the ceaseless Japanese advance. However, Wingate's arrival was too late as British military personnel at the Bush Warfare School had begun their long retreat to India. Calvert and Wingate would be reunited for Operation *Longcloth*, a long-range, deep penetration raid led by Brigadier Wingate in February 1943, utilizing the newly formed 77th Brigade, also known as the Chindits, in which Major Calvert was a column commander. (*USAMHI*)

(**Opposite page**) Australian infantry advance in a line abreast with an M3 Stuart light tank, getting only intermittent cover from the coconut trees of a plantation near Buna. A Bren gunner is firing his weapon from the hip since it was relatively lightweight for a machine-gun. General Douglas A. MacArthur's offensive along the northern Papuan coast in New Guinea by the Australians since the end of September 1942, along with the deployment of the US 32nd Infantry Division's battalions in November 1942, heralded an end to the myth of Japanese invincibility in the South-west Pacific Area (SWPA) of operations. Also, an Australian force had recently turned back a Japanese amphibious landing at Milne Bay on the eastern tip of Papua. (*Library of Congress*)

(**Above**) At Giropa Point near Buna, an Australian section leader climbs aboard an M3 light Stuart tank's hull to aid in directing the 37mm gunfire onto enemy pillboxes and positions on 2 January 1943. The M3 light tank, which had already demonstrated its obsolescence in North Africa, would show its utility in narrow jungle-clad trails of both New Guinea and the Solomon Islands. (*Library of Congress*)

(**Above**) The tide of the Imperial Japanese Army's *blitzkrieg* began to turn in late September 1942 after General Horii was ordered to end his overland advance on Port Moresby across the Owen Stanley Range in Papua, New Guinea because of an increasing commitment of Japanese resources to the fighting on Guadalcanal across the Solomon Sea to the east, after the US 1st Marine Division (Reinforced) had entrenched themselves and had control of the airfield, called Henderson Field, on Lunga Plain. Thereafter, the retreating Japanese troops were pursued by Australian forces and, then, by American infantry after the enemy retreated into their intricate defensive fortifications at Buna and Gona on Papua's northern coast. Above, across a waterway from Buna Mission, the crew of a 37mm antitank gun of the 128th US Infantry Regiment of the 32nd Division fires at Japanese pillboxes, which posed major obstacles to the Allied advance to recapture Papua. The fixed Japanese fortifications required artillery, aerial attack, direct tank gunfire and TNT satchels to destroy them. Allied casualties were exorbitantly high, convincing General MacArthur that there would be 'No More Bunas'. (*USAMHI*)

(**Opposite above**) American soldiers of the 32nd Infantry Division at Buna occupy a former Japanese fortified trench covered with dense foliage. The GIs brandish their M1 semi-automatic Garand rifles at the ready. Many of the Japanese positions were so well concealed that American infantry patrols would come under enemy fire from only a matter of yards. The destruction of Japan's northern Papuan bases at Buna and Gona marked another Allied turning point in the Pacific War. (*USAMHI*)

(**Opposite below**) Marines put out a fire in a Grumman F4F Wildcat near a hangar on Henderson Field. Note that some of the Marines are wearing side arms, since there was always a concern for the Japanese infiltrators breaking through the perimeter to get to their objective, the airstrip. By holding Henderson Field, the Americans had an unsinkable aircraft carrier in the south-eastern Solomon Sea. American possession of Guadalcanal would always be a threat to the Japanese strategy and installations in Papua, New Guinea. (*USMC*)

(**Above**) A 75mm pack Howitzer is positioned by a crew of the 11th Marines in a deep gun-pit lined with camouflaged-coloured sandbags. This weapon devastated Japanese infantry formations attempting to break through the Marine perimeter on numerous occasions, and thwarted the enemy's attempts to capture Henderson Field and compel the Americans to surrender, which would, once again, give Yamamoto control over all of the Solomon Islands and enable implementation of plans for further south-eastern expansion. Judging by the relatively thin bodies of the Marines in this gun-crew, it is evident food was not abundant during the initial months on the island, hence Guadalcanal's moniker, 'Starvation Island'. (USMC)

(**Opposite above**) District Officer Martin Clemens poses with his native scouts on Guadalcanal. Clemens, a Cambridge graduate and a captain commissioned in the British Army, was situated at Aola, the local seat of government before the war. On 28 May 1942, Clemens was made aware of a Japanese landing party surveying Lunga Plain and forwarded the information to Australia. Japanese Captain Shigetoshi Miyazaki's inspection party of the seaplane-equipped Yokohama Air Group stationed at Tulagi favourably reported Guadalcanal as a suitable installation for an advanced air-base in the southern Solomon Islands. From June to July 1942, more than 2,500 men of the 11th and 13th Construction Units landed at Lunga Point to build an airfield on Lunga Plain and were duly observed by Clemens and his native scouts. An eventual Japanese airfield on Guadalcanal was to protect the drive to Port Moresby in Papua, New Guinea, as well as cover the eventual IJN moves south-eastwards into the New Hebrides, Fiji and Tonga Island groups to sever the sea lanes between the United States and the Antipodes, thereby eliminating Australia and New Zealand as staging areas to reclaim the territory captured by the enemy. (USMC)

(**Opposite below**) The IJA suffered grievously on Guadalcanal with uncoordinated, piecemeal attacks that failed to breach the Marine perimeter and capture Henderson Field. Here, soldiers of the 2nd Battalion, 28th Infantry Regiment (the Ichiki Detachment), led by Colonel Kiyoano Ichiki, lay in grotesque postures of death in a sand-pit near the mouth of Alligator Creek. The Japanese were going to destroy American morale with a nocturnal, frontal bayonet charge. Marine rifle, machine-gun, 37mm antitank gunfire and artillery of the 11th Marines broke up the attack on the night of 21 August 1942. The next day, Marine M3 light Stuart tanks annihilated the survivors of the previous night's attack. Japanese tactics, such as these massed infantry charges, relied on *bushido* or the warrior code and would lead to heavy casualties and a failure to seize objectives throughout the South Pacific campaign. (NARA)

(**Above**) The wreck of the Japanese transport, the *Kinugawa Maru*, is beached along Guadalcanal's northern coast as a testimony to the defeat of the enemy in the southern Solomons in late 1942 to early 1943. Although the IJN inflicted grievous losses on both the American and Australian naval forces during the Guadalcanal campaign, the sinking or disabling of Japanese vessels prevented adequate resupply and reinforcement of the troops on the island. The prevention of Japanese resupply of island outposts with Allied air and naval assets was to become an emerging strategic paradigm for island-hopping victories throughout the South Pacific campaign. (*NARA*)

(**Opposite above**) An abandoned Japanese 90mm antitank gun and ammunition that was left behind by the retreating enemy at Kokumbona Beach is situated under its vegetation camouflage in late January 1943. Within several days, Japanese destroyers would evacuate several thousand of their soldiers from the western coast of Guadalcanal and redeploy them at their relatively new bases on New Georgia. (*NARA*)

(**Opposite below**) A beached Japanese landing barge or *Daihatsu* Type A near Kokumbona, after an American air attack, is shown. The Marine Dauntless SBD dive-bombers and P-400 fighter-bombers were especially effective at interdicting Japanese coastal supply and reinforcement traffic. Each of these Japanese barges could carry seventy troops or 12 tons of cargo or a medium tank. It is ironic that observation of these Japanese craft, with their lowered bow ramps in the sands along China's beaches, made by Marine lieutenant Victor H. 'Brute' Krulak in the late 1930s, when combined with the New Orleans boatyards of small boat-shipbuilder Andrew Jackson Higgins, would provide the US Navy with a class of watercraft called 'Higgins Boats'. These landing craft would be the instrument for the Allies to deliver assault waves, vehicles, supplies and reinforcements to hostile shores throughout the entire Pacific. Incidentally, Krulak led the 2nd Marine Parachute Battalion on an eleven-day raid of northern Choiseul Island as a diversion for Vice Admiral Halsey's major Bougainville amphibious assault of 1 November 1943. (*NARA*)

A Japanese gravesite with markers indicates the burial place of a dead infantryman after the battle of Kokumbona Beach on Guadalcanal in January 1943. Prior to the battle, the IJN floated supplies to wash ashore at this important trail hub, but action at Kokumbona Beach drove the enemy away. American air and naval patrols had severely interdicted Japanese resupply and reinforcements of the IJA troops on Guadalcanal, necessitating the emperor's agreement to draw-up plans for the evacuation of the southern Solomon Island. (*NARA*)

(**Opposite above**) An aerial view shows the completed Henderson Field complex after Guadalcanal was secured in February 1943. The challenge on Guadalcanal, as it would be for all of the island-hopping and coastal assaults through the South Pacific, would be to create or seize existing airfields in order to bring aerial attack closer to the enemy, usually in preparation of upcoming amphibious assaults or to isolate Japanese garrisons, such as Rabaul, by an overwhelming air interdiction of either enemy supply or evacuation. (*NARA*)

(**Opposite below**) A USAAF B-17 four-engine heavy bomber rests on Marston matting at Henderson Field. The placement of this steel planking enabled the B-17 heavy bombers to use the field as a way-station for long-range missions. Prior to that, aircraft of the 11th Heavy Bombardment Group under Colonel LaVerne Saunders, stationed at Espiritu Santo and Efate, 590 and 714 miles respectively from Guadalcanal in the New Hebrides Islands, were the only long-range bombers that could conduct missions over the southern Solomon Islands. Early on, the 11th Heavy Bombardment Group faced a shortage of planes, spare parts, replacement pilots and aircrew in addition to primitive conditions for the mechanics to work in. Eventually, the USAAF command ordered successive squadrons of the 5th Heavy Bombardment Group, stationed in Hawaii, to head for the South Pacific. To emphasize the need for airfield construction with Marston matting, Admiral Nimitz landed at Henderson Field on 30 September 1942, during a torrential rainstorm, that transformed the runway into a pool of mud and made for a harrowing experience. (*NARA*)

Vice Admiral William F. 'Bull' Halsey, Jr. (*left*) is sworn in as Commander-in-Chief, South Pacific, by his chief of staff, Captain Miles Browning, on 18 October 1942 amid some of the darkest hours of the American defence of Guadalcanal. Halsey replaced Vice Admiral Robert Ghormley, the latter having a pessimistic outlook about the feasibility of the Guadalcanal campaign that was launched on 7 August 1942. Halsey energized the troops on Guadalcanal by sending whatever supplies and reinforcements to the island that were at his disposal as well as vigorously contesting Japanese resupply and bombardment efforts with naval surface actions that produced extensive casualties among the ranks of his sailors. Halsey served aboard destroyers combating German submarines during the First World War. He held assignments in naval Intelligence and also served as naval attaché to the Weimar Republic in Berlin in 1922. He became intrigued by fleet aviation and in 1935, at the age of 52, received his aviator's wings. Prior to the Second World War, he commanded the USS *Saratoga* and, in 1940, received the rank of vice admiral and took command of the Pacific Aircraft Battle Force. (*NARA*)

(**Opposite above**) At Henderson Field on Guadalcanal bombs are brought to a US Navy Grumman TBF Avenger. The plane is parked atop the pierced Marston steel matting as it is prepared for a mission in the Central Solomon Islands. After a disastrous debut at the Battle of Midway in June 1942, the Avenger became the navy's major torpedo bomber during the remainder of the war. It had a crew of three with two forward-firing 0.5-inch calibre machine-guns and one 0.5-inch calibre rear-firing Browning machine-gun in the dorsal turret, as well as a 0.3-inch calibre rearward-firing machine-gun in the ventral position. The Avenger could carry a 2,500lb bomb-load. (*Author's Collection*)

(**Opposite below**) A Lockheed USAAF P-38 'Lightning' heavy fighter is readied for take-off for a sortie into the Central Solomons from Guadalcanal's Fighter One airstrip. It was a P-38 flown from Guadalcanal by USAAF Lieutenant Thomas Lanphier that shot down the IJN Combined Fleet Admiral Isoroku Yamamoto's transport plane, a twin-engined IJN Mitsubishi G4M3 'Betty' bomber, over southern Bougainville on the morning of 18 April 1943. The P-38 would become one of the most successful Allied interceptors in the Pacific as it possessed four M2 Browning 0.50-inch calibre machine-guns and one Hispano M1 20mm cannon in the plane's nose. It was capable of attaining a top speed of roughly 400 mph, making it considerably faster than any Japanese fighter in service, and performed exceptionally well above 20,000ft. The P-38's range was also superior to any of the other American fighters in the South Pacific, allowing it to make the round trip from Guadalcanal to Bougainville. The plane had a unique appearance with its twin booms located behind each turbo super-charged Allison engine and tricycle landing gear; one below each boom and the other below the aircraft's nose. (*NARA*)

US Navy Task Force (TF) 16, built around the carriers USS *Hornet* and *Enterprise*, among other cruisers and destroyers, was under the command of the audacious Halsey. Here, a USAAF twin-engined B-25B 'Mitchell' medium bomber, capable of delivering a 2,000lb bomb-load on Japan, takes off from the deck of the USS *Hornet* at 0820 hours on 18 April 1942. Halsey ordered the attack earlier than planned after TF 16 was sighted by the Japanese. The *Hornet*, under the direct command of Captain Marc A. Mitscher, was on her initial voyage, delivering the 16 B-25Bs from the 17th Bombardment Group, under Lieutenant Colonel James H. Doolittle, as a strike-force halfway around the world from its embarkation point at Norfolk, Virginia, to the northern Pacific launch site. The technique of a medium bomber taking off from a rolling carrier deck was perfected by army pilots prior to Halsey's task force leaving for the raid. In all, the entire launch sequence took just over an hour. (*NARA*)

Lieutenant General Haruyoshi Hyakutake, commander of the IJA 17th Army, stands at his headquarters at Rabaul. Hyakutake had the misfortune of having to conduct IJA operations both in Papua and on Guadalcanal simultaneously. This operational dilemma compelled him to withdraw his overland Port Moresby attacking force and take up defensive positions at Buna and Gona, in order to reinforce Guadalcanal after failed infantry assault setbacks to capture Henderson Field in August and September 1942. Hyakutake would later command the Japanese 17th Army on Bougainville in 1943–1945. In early October, at Kahili on Bougainville, he would be unceremoniously carried in a makeshift sedan chair to a landing barge to take him to a Japanese high-ranking officers stockade. (*NARA*)

(**Left**) Commander of the Japanese Combined Fleet, Admiral Isoruku Yamamoto, is shown in a formal portrait. The IJN was to lead in the defence of the Solomon Islands after the evacuation of Guadalcanal in early February 1943. To augment his forces at Rabaul and at Buin on Bougainville, Yamamoto moved roughly 200 carrier planes to shore-based facilities in order to attack the American installations on Guadalcanal and Tulagi in April 1943. He strengthened his new airfields as well at Munda on New Georgia and Vila on Kolombangara Island just to the north-west of the former base, anticipating that the Central Solomons would be Halsey's next target. On the morning of 18 April 1943, one year after the Doolittle Raid on Tokyo, Yamamoto's personal bomber, which was taking him to Bougainville and another offshore islet base at Ballale, was shot down by US Army P-38 fighters stationed at Henderson Field on Guadalcanal. Yamamoto's charred remains were later found in the jungle. (*Author's Collection*)

(**Right**) General Hitoshi Imamura is shown in a formal portrait. Situated at Rabaul, Imamura, was the general officer commanding the 8th Area Army, which had operational control over the 17th Japanese Army and 6th Division on Bougainville. Early in the war, Imamura commanded the Japanese 16th Army in the conquest of the Netherland East Indies and managed to survive the sinking of his transport during the invasion of Java. On 9 November 1942, at the height of the battle for Guadalcanal, he was given command of the 8th Area Army, based at Rabaul. In this capacity, he commanded both the 17th and the 18th Armies during operations in the Solomons and New Guinea respectively. He was promoted to full general in May 1943. Convicted of atrocities committed by troops under his command, he was imprisoned until 1954. (*NARA*)

(**Above**) Two Marines inspect a destroyed Japanese Mitsubishi A6M Reisen 'Zero' on a Guadalcanal beach. The Marine Grumman F4F Wildcat fighter pilots had to learn from bitter experience how to deal with these more manoeuvrable Japanese fighters. In the end, pilot armour and self-sealing fuel tanks in the Wildcats enabled them to take a much greater punishment than their adversaries. Also, the Marine pilots were flying above their home airfield, while the battle-damaged Japanese fighters had to make it back to Rabaul prior to the airfields at Munda Point on New Georgia, Vila Point on Kolombangara and Buin on Bougainville being completely operational. (*USAMHI*)

(**Opposite above**) A flight of A6M3 Model 22 Reisens or 'Zeroes' with external fuel tanks flies over the Solomon Islands in 1943. The term 'Zero' refers to the Japanese term Reisen, which indicates the Japanese year 2600, or 1940, when the plane was adopted by the IJN. It was a superb carrier-borne or land-based single-seat fighter. When the aircraft made its debut as a carrier-borne fighter, it quickly achieved parity or superiority with any of the other combatant nations' land-based fighters. These A6M3 aircraft had more power than earlier models. However, the range was shorter. Nonetheless, when fitted with external fuel tanks, as shown, the A6M3 had a phenomenal range of approximately 2,000 miles, enabling them to fly from Rabaul on New Britain to escort bombers to attack Guadalcanal and Tulagi. (*Author's Collection*)

(**Opposite below**) The Japanese 8th Fleet Staff is photographed at Buin on Bougainville's south-eastern coast in May 1943. The IJN had several hundred men stationed there and another roughly 7,000 Special Naval Landing Force (SNLF) troops at the No.1 Base Headquarters at nearby Shortland Bay. The strong Japanese troop strength on Bougainville was to achieve the island's strategic objective as the most north-western and largest of the Solomon Islands – namely to help protect Rabaul. As such, the IJA had also stationed 15,000 Japanese troops of the 17th Army and 6th Division in the Buin area. (*Author's Collection*)

Japanese A6M3 Reisen or 'Zero' fighters prepare for take-off from Rabaul in late 1942. Lakunai airdrome, on the opposite side of Matupit Harbor (also referred to as *Rabingikku* by the Japanese), was established as the main base for the IJN fighters. Hundreds of revetments were built to protect the planes. Another airfield complex, Vunakanau, was also expanded with a paved concrete runway for IJN bombers and fighters. (*NARA*)

An IJA Nakajima Ki-43 Hayabusa ('Peregrine Falcon') or 'Oscar' single-seat fighter is parked at a landing field in 1942. The Ki-43 was considered the IJA's best fighter in terms of manoeuvrability and speed. Initially, it went into service lacking pilot armour, self-sealing gas tanks, or a starter motor, as well as light armament comprised of only two 12.7mm machine-guns. However, after encounters with more advanced Allied fighters, armour and self-sealing fuel tanks were added. The Ki-43 was deployed in greater numbers than any of the other IJA fighters and was second to only the A6M 'Zero' in terms of sheer production numbers. (*Author's Collection*)

IJN fighter pilots are briefed before a mission over the Southern Solomon Islands in early 1943 as part of Admiral Yamamoto's renewed aerial assault on American installations on Guadalcanal and Tulagi. The intensity of aerial combat in the skies over Guadalcanal during the peak of the struggle for that island, as well as the previous setbacks at the Battles of Coral Sea and Midway, had severely thinned the ranks of this excellent fleet air arm's cadre.
(Author's Collection)

A USAAF twin-engined B-25 'Mitchell' bomber from General Kenney's 5th Air Force in Papua strikes at a Japanese merchant vessel in Simpson Harbor at Rabaul on 2 November 1943. In the background, smoke billows from the wharves, jetties and ground installations as a result of the bombing. General Kenney was an innovator at using his twin-engined bombers to inflict extreme punishment on Japanese shipping and ground installations. Vital to these emerging air doctrinal tactics, Major Paul 'Pappy' Gunn, one of Kenney's officers, rearmed his B-25, along with his Douglas A-20 bombers, with an array of heavy forward firing nose machine-guns and cannon to strafe the enemy in a devastating manner from low altitude. The Douglas A-20 or 'Havoc' attack bomber was the American version of the three-seat light bomber initially bought by France and Britain and known by the British as the 'Boston' light bomber.
(Author's Collection)

(**Above**) Vice Admiral William F. Halsey (*second from left*) meets with some of his subordinates aboard the USS *Nassau* at his headquarters in Noumea, New Caledonia, on 24 December 1942. Operations to secure all of north-western Guadalcanal were underway and preliminary discussions as to the next objective were commencing. About six weeks after the Japanese evacuation from Guadalcanal, on 23 March 1943, the joint chiefs of staff in Washington announced their plans for a reduction of the Japanese fortress of Rabaul. There would be no direct amphibious invasion of that bastion at the north-eastern end of New Britain. Instead, Allied assault forces under MacArthur's South-west Pacific Area (SWPA) command and Halsey's South Pacific Force would move along the northern coast of New Guinea and through the Central and Northern Solomons respectively, culminating in landings to seize airfields on western New Britain and capture Bougainville to construct new runways. This plan was code-named Operation *Cartwheel*. From all of these airfields, Allied aeronautical might would isolate Rabaul by air interdiction only, turning it into a vast 'jungle prison camp'. (*Author's Collection*)

(**Opposite page**) Admiral Chester Nimitz, Commander-in-Chief Pacific Fleet (*left*) confers with Vice Admiral William Halsey aboard the USS *Curtiss* at Espiritu Santo in the New Hebrides Islands shortly before the Japanese evacuation from Guadalcanal. On the evening of 15 October 1942, Nimitz realized that he required a more aggressive commander for the South Pacific theatre, in order to turn around the poor situation among the Marines and aviators on Guadalcanal. In addition to the change of commanders of the South Pacific Force, Nimitz was able to get the US Army's 25th Infantry Division deployed from Hawaii to the Solomon Islands as well as more army fighters to reinforce the Marine contingents at Henderson Field. After Guadalcanal, Nimitz was in charge of operations in the Central Pacific, which would constitute a new front apart from Halsey's South Pacific and General MacArthur's SWPA commands. The three Pacific theatres would now compete for American war *matériel*, the production of which had still not peaked. (*NARA*)

(**Above**) General Douglas A. MacArthur (*left*) and General Sir Thomas Blamey (*far right*) are shown at the front, along the Kokoda Trail, in Papua in October 1942. During the dark days of the summer of 1942, the American chief of staff, General George C. Marshall, wanted Australian and Dutch officers to be included on MacArthur's senior staff in Australia. Blamey was recalled from his command of Australian forces in the Middle East to become Commander-in-Chief (C-in-C) Australian Military Forces (AMF) in Australia. MacArthur begrudgingly accepted Blamey but also ignored him. All eleven major MacArthur headquarters' assignments would be American, including eight senior officers that their leader had brought with him from Bataan and Corregidor. During the Japanese offensive down the Kokoda Trail, which reached a crisis point in mid-to-late September, MacArthur had begun making condescending and pejorative remarks about the *élan* of Australian troops and their commanders fighting the Japanese. At times, Blamey was to be in conflict with MacArthur's egocentric will and one day he admitted, 'the best and the worst things you hear about him [MacArthur] are both true'. In late 1944–1945, Blamey would be in overall command of Australian forces fighting on Bougainville in the Northern Solomons following the American departure. (*USAMHI*)

(**Opposite above**) A C-46 of the Air Transport Command (ATC) flies over the treacherous 'Hump' above the snow-capped Himalayas on a path from the air depots of Assam, India, to China's sout-western Yunnan Province's air terminals. This northerly, fuel-inefficient and dangerous route was used to avoid interdicting Japanese fighters based at Myitkyina. The China-Burma-India (CBI) theatre would consume an inordinate number of tons of Lend-Lease supplies to keep China in the war against Japan on the Asian mainland. (*NARA*)

(**Opposite below**) Lieutenant General Stilwell, the infantry trainer and tactician (*centre with campaign hat*), observes Chinese troops practising their artillery skills at his Ramgarh, India depot and facility. The hard training of the guns' crews would pay off in northern Burma's Hukawng Valley, where 75mm pack and 105mm Howitzers would be utilized to break stalemates with elements of the Japanese 18th Division in their bunkered positions, in December 1943–January 1944. (*USMAHI*)

(**Above**) Chinese troops cross over a bamboo suspension bridge on their trek from the Ramgarh training facility across the Indo-Burmese border into the Hukawng Valley, to combat elements of General Tanaka's 18th Division in northern Burma in late autumn 1943. Like all theatre commanders beginning their long-awaited offensives, Stilwell clamoured for more supplies and men. However, he was at the end of a long supply chain with at least three other actively competing ground combat theatres in the Pacific War. (*NARA*)

(**Opposite above**) Lieutenant General Stilwell, who preferred being at the front with his troops rather than back in India or Chunking in China, rides in a short column of Jeeps through a shallow stream in northern Burma while his force campaigns down the Hukawng and Mogaung valleys. He wears his iconic campaign hat and carries his trademark M1 carbine rifle. Known for his salty language and Anglophobic temperament, Stilwell would often vent his frustrations into his personal diary. Such was the fate of all the theatre commanders, including Halsey and MacArthur, who continually groused about not getting enough war *matériel* for their offensives. (*USAMHI*)

(**Opposite below**) Brigadier General Lewis Pick (*left*), head of the Ledo Road and pipeline project, views progress on the construction with Admiral Lord Louis Mountbatten, commander South East Asia Command (SEAC), among other British officers, at Ledo on 7 April 1944. In addition to the Ledo Road, Pick, along with Major General Raymond Wheeler (Commanding General, Services of Supply, CBI), would also construct two oil pipelines from Indian refineries via Ledo to Myitkyina. (*NARA*)

(**Opposite page**) A truck convoy halts along the Ledo Road by a mudslide. Drainage of the road was a persistent problem, as evidenced by a piece of culvert tube lying to the left of the road surface. The construction of the Ledo Road and the combat to liberate northern Burma of the Japanese were enormous drains on American war production, as campaigns were simultaneously being waged in other theatres. Some cynics would contend that the Stilwell Road overland supply route from India to China had become obsolete as, by the end of January 1945, the Allied war planners had decided to attack the Japanese Home Islands directly through the Central Pacific and Philippines rather than from the Chinese mainland or Formosa. (*USAMHI*)

(**Above**) British Major General Orde C. Wingate (*left*) and USAAF Colonel Philip Cochran (*right*), brief British pilots at Hailakandi airfield in India in March 1944 prior to Operation *Thursday*, which comprised a larger Chindit long-range deep airborne penetration operation with the 3rd Indian Division (also called Special Force) in northern Burma to assist Stilwell's ground offensive. Wingate, Cochran and USAAF Colonel John Alison (not shown) revolutionized long-range penetration warfare with a myriad aircraft utilizing creative tactics dreamed up by the triumvirate. Wingate's new doctrine for this mission was dependent on Cochran and Alison's 1st Air Commando Group, which would furnish all the transport as well as parachute resupply, in addition to providing 'aerial artillery' for the Chindit brigades. This novel aerial dimension allowed Wingate to exist behind enemy lines without any land or sea lines of communication. Also, with the construction of rough, local airfields as well as larger positions called 'strongholds', timely casualty evacuation could be accomplished. (*NARA*)

At Hsamshingyang in northern Burma in early April 1944, Brigadier General Frank Merrill (*centre*), commander of the 5307th Composite Unit (Provisional), also known by the moniker Merrill's Marauders, reviews plans with his US Army Nisei-Japanese interpreters, Staff Sergeants Herb Miyazaki (*left*) and Akiji Yoshimura (*right*). The remaining marauders, along with Chinese regiments and Kachin irregulars led by American officers and infantrymen from the Office of Strategic Services (OSS) Detachment 101, would capture the Japanese-held airfield at Myitkyina in a *coup de main*, led by Marauder Colonel Charles Hunter, on 17 May 1944. (*NARA*)

Chapter Two

Stepping-Stones After Guadalcanal

Australian coastwatchers

A number of Australians served as coastwatchers after being recruited by Lieutenant Commander Eric Feldt of the Royal Australian Navy (RAN), who was placed in charge of intelligence-gathering for New Guinea and the Solomon Islands. This organization had a control station called KEN, which corresponded to the radio call letters it utilized. The signals station was located on Guadalcanal and situated near Henderson Field as of October 1942. The KEN station was established by Lieutenant Commander Hugh MacKenzie, Eric Feldt's deputy for the area, and it coordinated coastwatcher activity throughout the Solomon Islands.

Some of the more notable of the Australian coastwatchers included Lieutenant Commander W.J. 'Jack' Read, RAN, who before the war was an assistant district officer stationed on the northern end of Bougainville near Buka Island. Read, who remained on Japanese-occupied Bougainville from August 1942 onwards, would send very brief radio signals to Guadalcanal alerting the Marines of impending aerial or naval attacks coming down 'The Slot' from Rabaul. The reason for the brevity of his messages was his concern of Japanese radio-detection equipment on Bougainville.

Major Donald G. Kennedy ran the coastwatcher compound and supervised an armed native constabulary at Segi Point, on New Georgia's eastern tip. As a district officer for the Central Solomon Islands, he was intimately knowledgeable with the entire area. He had originally been stationed on Santa Isabel Island, to the north-east of New Georgia Island. When the Japanese arrived, he relocated to Segi Point, where the approaches to his location were much more protected. There, Kennedy transformed the old Markham Plantation into a coastwatching and native scout base, defended with emplaced Japanese machine-guns that had been captured from the enemy. Kennedy's base at Segi Point also included an arsenal and a prisoner-of-war cage. Kennedy and his natives were vital at rescuing downed Allied pilots and capturing those of the enemy, the latter having their aircraft damaged in the skies over Guadalcanal. In February 1943, Admiral Yamamoto unleashed his Rabaul-based bombers with fighter escort on American installations on both Guadalcanal and

Tulagi after the Japanese evacuation following the brutal six-month campaign. In addition to having a reputation of being the best radio repairman in the Solomons, Kennedy also routinely conducted ambushes on small Japanese patrols that were sent to hunt him down and shut down his base of operations.

Another coastwatcher was Lieutenant A.R. (Reg) Evans, Royal Australian Navy Volunteer Reserve (RANVR). Evans enlisted in the Australian Imperial Force (AIF) during the early days of the Second World War, before transferring to the RANVR. From those ranks, Feldt brought him into his coastwatcher organization. Before the war, Evans was a purser on a steamer in the Solomons and knew the island chain well. In February 1943, Evans was an assistant at the KEN station on Guadalcanal, working under MacKenzie. The next month, Evans was dispatched to Kolombangara Island to set-up a separate station there. So, in late March 1943, Evans left Kennedy's Segi Point coastwatcher compound and landed on Kolombangara to observe the Japanese building an airfield at Vila to support their large airdrome at Munda Point on New Georgia Island. In the spring of 1943, KEN sent Evans an assistant, US Army Corporal Frank Nash, who had experience with radio signals equipment. Nash was to become the only American coastwatcher behind enemy lines in the Solomon Islands. Nash, a former cattle-rancher from Colorado, managed to join the KEN operation on Guadalcanal in April 1943 and a month later was moving through the Central Solomon Islands by canoe to join Evans. As an aside, Evans was credited as being instrumental in saving future American president Lieutenant (Junior Grade) John F. Kennedy and the survivors of his PT-109 crew, after their boat was rammed by the Japanese destroyer *Amagiri* in Blackett Strait on 2 August 1943 attempting to interdict enemy destroyer traffic from Rabaul (the 'Tokyo Express') bringing rein-forcements to Vila and Munda airfields on Kolombangara and New Georgia Islands respectively.

From the onset of Halsey's South Pacific campaign in 1943, the vital importance of having Australian coastwatchers to provide intelligence from areas behind the Japanese lines in the Central Solomons was recognized. So when plans were made to invade New Georgia and the other Central Solomon Islands, a constant stream of radio transmissions emanated from New Georgia, Vella Lavella, Kolombangara and Rendova Islands.

After fifteen months of Japanese occupation, Bougainville's native Melanesian population was thoroughly pro-Japanese. The Allies were unable to ascertain current intelligence about Japanese movements since many of the coastwatchers had been captured and those still at large were unable to move around the island safely. By July 1943, most of the Allied coastwatchers, not in captivity or executed, were evacuated from Bougainville. The Japanese knew that an eventual battle for Bougainville was going to be more crucial than the previous losing struggle for Guadalcanal.

The Russell Islands (Operation *Cleanslate*)

Before the attack on the New Georgia group of islands in the Central Solomons could be mounted, the Russell Islands, 35 miles north-west of Cape Esperance on Guadalcanal's western coast, would have to be seized. On 7 February 1943, the day the Japanese left Guadalcanal, Halsey's South Pacific Force was ordered to invade those islands. Halsey's intelligence staff was of the belief that there were 5,000–6,000 Japanese troops in those islands and, in order to safely maintain Guadalcanal and Henderson Field, his main base with over 300 aeroplanes to assault the Japanese in the Central and Northern Solomons, he decided to launch an amphibious assault to clear them from the Russell Islands. On 9 February, as Rear Admiral R. Kelly Turner was assembling his invasion force at Guadalcanal, word came that the Japanese had evacuated the Russell Islands. Nonetheless, Turner's ships left Lunga Roads at Guadalcanal on the night of 20 February and without incident, except for a badly coordinated Japanese IJN twin-engined, land-based Mitsubishi G4M3 'Betty' torpedo bomber attack, reached the Russell Islands by dawn in an anti-climactic manner. On 21 February, the 3rd Marine Raider Battalion, led by Lieutenant Colonel Harry B. Liversedge, landed on Pavuvu, and the US 43rd Infantry Division landed on Banika. The Marine 11th Defense Battalion also landed on Banika on 21 February and had its anti-aircraft emplacements operations that same day. Over the next week, an additional 9,000 US troops were brought to the islands to build an air-base on Banika and naval facilities for PT boats and other surface craft. US Navy Construction Battalions, the 'Seabees', had the first of two new airstrips operational on Banika by 15 April 1943.

The New Georgia Island Group: Rendova and sites proximate to Munda Airfield (Operation *Toenails*)

After securing Guadalcanal and the Russell Islands, the Allies could now attack Kolombangara and New Georgia Island from both the sea and air without much difficulty. Halsey's strategists planned for the seizure of Rendova, an island directly south across Blanche Channel from Munda Point, where a strong Japanese air-base had been developed. Rendova would serve as an excellent locale to shell Munda Airfield with 105mm Howitzers and the longer-range 155mm 'Long Tom' M1A1 cannon. Yamamoto had been building airfields and compelled the IJA to provide roughly 10,000 protective garrison troops at Vila and Munda Point in the New Georgia group as well as at Ballale, an islet off of the southern coast of Bougainville in the Northern Solomons. It was now obvious to the Japanese high command that with an air-base in the Russells, Allied aircraft could easily target both New Georgia and Kolombangara. Indeed, Munda airfield came under marauding US Navy destroyer gunfire as early as 4 March 1943.

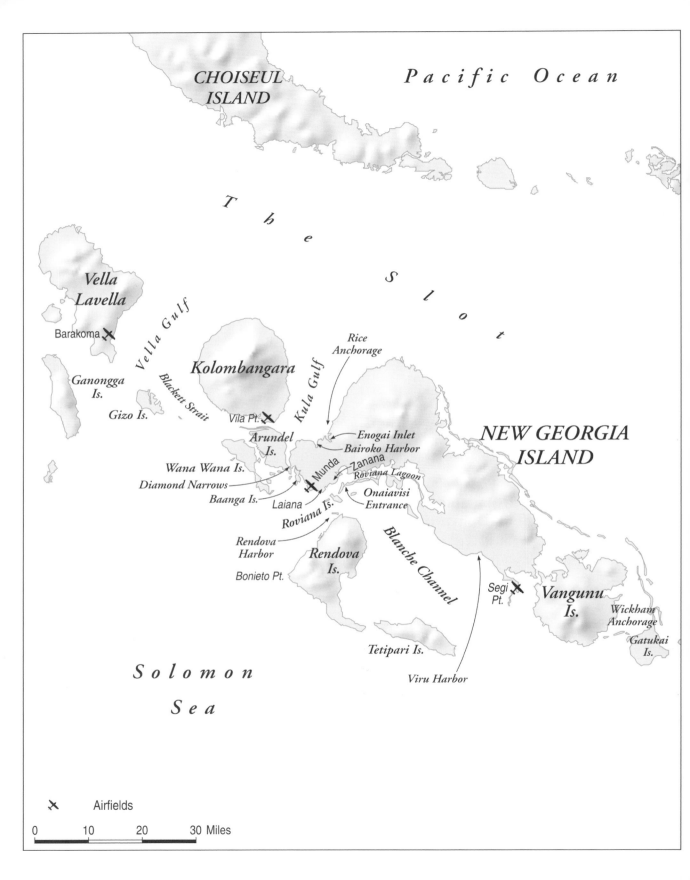

CHOISEUL
ISLAND

Pacific Ocean

T h e

S l o t

*Vella
Lavella*

Barakoma ✕

Vella Gulf

*Ganongga
Is.*

Blackett Strait

Gizo Is.

Kolombangara

Kula Gulf

Rice
Anchorage

Vila Pt. ✕

*Arundel
Is.*

Enogai Inlet
Bairoko Harbor

**NEW GEORGIA
ISLAND**

Wana Wana Is.

✕✕ Munda
Zanana

Diamond Narrows

Roviana Lagoon

Baanga Is.

Laiana

*Onaiavisi
Entrance*

Roviana Is.

*Rendova
Harbor*

*Rendova
Is.*

Blanche Channel

Bonieto Pt.

Segi
Pt. ✕

*Vangunu
Is.*

*Wickham
Anchorage*

*Gatukai
Is.*

Solomon

Tetipari Is.

Sea

Viru Harbor

✕   Airfields

0   10   20   30 Miles

The Central Solomons offensive would involve the heavily reinforced US 43rd Infantry Division, which would be transported from both Guadalcanal and the Russell Islands to secure tactical vantage points at four locales for the eventual invasion of New Georgia and capture of Munda Airfield. Separate landing forces would embark for Rendova Island, with its barrier islets and harbour. Rendova was to be transformed into a PT boat base and a forward artillery fire base to shell Munda. The other three sites deemed necessary to occupy for the eventual seizure of Munda Airfield included Segi Point, on the south-eastern end of New Georgia, Viru Harbor, a Japanese base up the southern coast of New Georgia from Segi Point, and Wickham Anchorage, a well-situated sheltered harbour, garrisoned by the Japanese, off Vangunu Island.

The landing at Segi Point was launched in response to fears of a looming large Japanese assault there, utilizing the entire 1st Battalion/229th IJA Infantry Regiment. The Japanese objectives were to seize Major Kennedy's compound and build their own airfield at Segi Point. However, Halsey's planners also wanted a fighter strip to be built by the US Navy Construction Battalions or 'Seabees' at Segi Point. An airstrip at Segi Point would minimize the distances Halsey's planes would have to fly on

Map 2. In late June 1943, Halsey's South Pacific Force began the invasion of the Central Solomon Islands with the main objective being the capture of Munda Airfield on New Georgia Island's south-western tip. A Marine raider battalion detachment plus some American soldiers landed at Segi Point on 20–21 June to protect a coastwatcher's compound and future airfield site there. This Marine raider battalion then moved up the coast onto Viru Harbor on 30 June, where it overwhelmed the Japanese garrison within twenty-four hours of sharp fire-fights. A smaller landing at Wickham Anchorage, which separates the south-eastern coast of Vangunu Island from the smaller Gatukai Island, was made by army infantry units accompanied by some Marine raiders on 30 June against a small Japanese garrison. A fuel station and staging area for PT boats and other small craft moving north through 'The Slot' from Guadalcanal and the Russells would be situated there. Also on 30 June, an amphibious landing to capture Rendova Island commenced just before dawn at that island's North Point near Rendova Harbor. From 3–5 July, New Georgia Occupation Force (NGOF) was ferried from Rendova to New Georgia's Zanana Beach. To assist isolating Munda Airfield from Japanese reinforcements via Kolombangara, a separate Marine raider–army landing force occupied Rice Anchorage on 4–5 July in order to seize Bairoko Harbor after occupying Enogai Inlet. By 5 August, the tenacious Japanese defence and jungle fighting for the Munda area ceased with extensive 'mopping-up' operations on New Georgia and Munda airstrip repair to commence. Baanga Island, off New Georgia's Dragon Peninsula, was attacked by army units on 10 August and secured after ten days of combat, with the few Japanese survivors escaping to Arundel and Kolombangara Islands. Arundel Island was invaded by army units on 27 August, but major reinforcements were required to secure it from fanatical Japanese resistance by 21 September. Halsey did not want another protracted campaign to capture the Vila airstrip on Kolombangara Island, so it was decided to bypass this heavily defended island and prevent its resupply by naval and aerial interdiction. As a prelude to moving into the Northern Solomons, Halsey would instead seize the lightly held island of Vella Lavella, 15 miles to the north-west of Kolombangara. On 15 August, Marine, army and US Navy 'Seabee' units landed unopposed at Barakoma. Progress at securing Vella Lavella was slow, so Halsey landed elements of the 3rd New Zealand Division on 18 September to force the enemy's evacuation of the island within a week. Ultimately, the Japanese in the Central Solomons were evacuated to Choiseul and Bougainville Islands to the north and north-west, respectively. (*Philip Schwartzberg, Meridian Mapping*)

missions to the Central Solomons from their current airfields at Guadalcanal and from a newly constructed one in the Russell Islands. Thus, a detachment of the 4th Marine Raider Battalion was landed at Segi Point by US Navy destroyers on 20–21 June 1943. The Marines' assignments were to protect both Kennedy's base and to hold the area from further Japanese encroachment as the enemy was situated at both Viru Harbor to the west and Wickham Anchorage to the east. Additional soldiers of the 1st Battalion, 103rd US Infantry Regiment were prepared to assist the Marines, if needed, to maintain possession of Segi Point for the future-planned American airfield there. These units were part of Halsey's Eastern Landing Force.

As no major encounter occurred, this raider detachment, from the 4th Raider Battalion, was then to move to Viru Harbor, through intense rain and thick mud, and attack the Japanese installation there on 30 June. After some fire-fights and a failed Japanese *banzai* charge by the roughly 250 men of the IJA 229th Infantry Regiment, the Marine raiders captured the enemy compound at Viru. After ferreting out snipers and some surviving Japanese in the New Georgia jungle, they turned the area over to army troops. The rest of the Japanese garrison took jungle trails back to Munda. By 1 July 1943, Viru Harbor with its naval shore-gun along with the garrison ceased being an issue for Halsey's subsequent movements.

Temporally coincident with the beginning of the Central Solomons campaign with the Rendova landings was a smaller one at Wickham Anchorage on 30 June on the south-east coast of Vangunu Island, which is situated between the south-eastern end of New Georgia Island and the much smaller Gatukai Island. This would become a fuel station for PT boats and other small craft moving north through 'The Slot' from Guadalcanal.

Halsey's main amphibious operation on 30 June was with his Western Landing Force assaulting Rendova during intense tropical rain at that island's North Point. Elements of the US 169th Infantry Regiment also seized two smaller barrier islands, Bau and Kokorana, against no resistance in order to keep Blanche Channel's approach to Rendova Harbor open. The US 43rd Infantry Division's 172nd Regimental Combat Team's (RCT) 3,500 men and a battalion of the 103rd Infantry Regiment landing at Rendova faced no more than 400 Japanese in a series of fire-fights and, at times, hand-to-hand combat. The Japanese troops were from the 3rd Battalion/229th IJA Infantry Regiment and a company of the Kure 6th SNLF. The US Navy warships accompanying the transports silenced some Japanese artillery batteries on Munda Cape firing on them during the early morning hours. A few of the enemy escaped in an attempt to reach Munda. As the soldiers of the 172nd RCT moved inland from the beachhead on 1 July, the Marine 9th Defense Battalion began erecting anti-aircraft emplacements for their 90mm anti-aircraft (AA) guns as well as 40mm Bofors guns along with 20mm and .50-inch calibre AA machine-guns in and around the Rendova Plantation.

The predictable Japanese aerial counter-attack, however, with only IJN Zero fighters from Rabaul, ensued that morning with Allied fighters dispatched from Guadalcanal protecting the invasion fleet without a loss of any surface ship. Another late afternoon Japanese air attack with both twin-engined Mitsubishi G4M3 'Betty' torpedo bombers and fighters disabled Admiral Turner's command transport the USS *McCawley*, which was later inadvertently sunk that night, probably by torpedoes from an American PT boat. During the next few days, Japanese air attacks would inflict 150 casualties on Americans at the Rendova beachhead as well as destroy several landing craft and pieces of equipment. Japanese cruisers and destroyers would also sneak through 'The Slot' at night to harass the beachhead. Nonetheless, the success of the Rendova landings had been complete. Soon long-range artillery would be placed in position to shell Munda Airfield. However, the Marines and soldiers on Rendova would have to contend with the tenacious mud that the ceaseless rain had produced as well as the numerous tree-top level Japanese air attacks. Rendova Island was secured on 4 July. Halsey's staff had hoped that after four days on Rendova, sufficient men and material would have been concentrated for an assault across Roviana Lagoon to Zanana Beach on 4–5 July, thereby, undertaking a direct invasion of New Georgia Island closer to Munda Airfield with a large-scale force.

A Marine landing craft approaches one of the Russell Islands, 80 miles away from the north-western tip of Guadalcanal, unopposed on 20 February 1943. The assault boat crews were vigilant at their machine-guns, as Japanese air attacks were always likely. (*NARA*)

Marine raiders in an inflatable rubber boat approach one of the islands in the Russell group north-west of Guadalcanal on 20 February 1943. The original raider battalions were trained to paddle these craft in order to land silently without alerting the enemy on their myriad missions. However, some had outboard motors to assist movement. In this photograph, the lead Marine is aiming his Browning Automatic Rifle (BAR) as the inflatable boat approaches the shore while the other Marines have their rifles slung while paddling. (*USMC*)

(**Opposite page**) On constant alert for enemy snipers, three Marines scout the interior of one of the Russell Islands, although it was widely believed that the Japanese had withdrawn to the Central Solomons. The Marines are walking through coconut palms and are spread out on this patrol. (*USMC*)

(**Below**) After securing the Russell Islands, these soldiers leisurely unload a Landing Craft Mechanized (LCM) and stack ammunition piles as others watch. An airstrip was to be built and defended on the Russell Islands to bring American air power closer to Japanese installations in the Central and Northern Solomon Islands. (*NARA*)

(**Above**) A US Navy ferry, laden with supplies, trucks and scout cars, crosses Renard Sound between two of the Russell Islands. In addition to the US Navy 'Seabees' constructing an airfield, numerous trails would have to be widened within the coconut groves to allow for vehicular movement. (*NARA*)

(**Opposite above**) American soldiers, part of the 9,000 troops landed in the Russell Islands by Rear Admiral R. Kelly Turner, move inland without opposition. GIs from the US 148th Infantry Regiment of the 37th Division would be stationed on Banika Island in the Russell Islands before being deployed to Rendova and New Georgia in the Central Solomon Islands. Soldiers from the 43rd Infantry Division's 103rd Regiment landed in the Russell Islands on 21 February 1943 without opposition and were engaged in construction and training. The regiment was later deployed to Segi Point on New Georgia on 20–21 June 1943 along with Marine raiders to defend the site there for airfield construction. (*NARA*)

(**Opposite below**) The crew of a Marine 90mm anti-aircraft (AA) gun in its reinforced emplacement loads a shell into the weapon's breech to fire at Japanese bombers overhead. Japanese Admiral Yamamoto had renewed his air attacks on Guadalcanal and Tulagi during the late winter of 1943 and the Russell Islands, as a more advanced staging area, were also targeted. (*NARA*)

(**Opposite above**) A Marine R4D (the equivalent to a USAAF C-47) takes off from a newly built airstrip in the Russell Islands past a defensive 40mm Bofors gun. The airstrip enabled Halsey's South Pacific fighter aircraft and light bombers to be in greater proximity to the Japanese fortified installations in the Central and Northern Solomon Islands. (*NARA*)

(**Above**) Marine raiders stationed in the Russell Islands after the unopposed landing unload a Japanese 37mm Type 94 rapid-fire artillery piece with shield from a captured landing barge or *daihatsu* left behind by the enemy when they evacuated the island group. This gun was originally designed to reduce enemy machine-gun nests. However, since much of Japan's artillery was obsolete by Western combatant nation standards, it also had to be utilized as the main Japanese anti-tank (AT) gun in all theatres until the war's end. (*NARA*)

(**Opposite below**) A US Navy Lockheed PV-1 'Ventura' (also called a B-34 'Lexington' by the USAAF) twin–engine bomber takes off from the newly completed airfield in the Russell Islands for a sortie against Japanese targets in the Central Solomons. This aircraft also served as a patrol plane in all theatres. Originally, the Lockheed Ventura was built to replace the older Lockheed Hudson bomber/patrol plane, the latter having fared poorly against the Japanese in the skies over Malaya. The plane had a crew of six and a range of over 1,600 miles with a service ceiling of 26,000 feet. It mounted four .50-inch calibre and two .30-inch calibre Browning machine-guns, in addition to carrying a 3,000lb bomb-load, one torpedo or six depth charges. In the South Pacific, the Royal New Zealand Air Force (RNZAF) flew these aircraft from fields in Fiji prior to missions from Henderson Field and the Russell Islands (as shown here), while the Australians flew them over New Guinea along with the more famous B-25 Mitchell bombers. (*NARA*)

(**Opposite page**) Soldiers of the 172nd Infantry Regiment, 43rd US Infantry Division, climb down cargo nets of the USS *McCawley* into landing craft for the assault on Rendova on 30 June 1943. The *McCawley*, Rear Admiral R. Kelly Turner's flagship, was later disabled in a Japanese air attack and inadvertently sunk by torpedoes, probably from an American PT boat. (*NARA*)

(**Above**) Landing craft circle to form an assault wave for Rendova Island in the New Georgia group on 30 June 1943. These troops were part of General Hester's Western Landing Force that would reach Rendova Point via Blanche Channel, which separated the larger island of New Georgia from the assault beaches. (*NARA*)

(**Below**) American landing craft with assault troops from the 172nd Infantry Regiment, US 43rd Division, prepare to hit the beach on Rendova Island on 30 June 1943. They would land there unopposed during heavy rain squalls. (*NARA*)

(**Opposite above**) As GIs scamper up the assault beach at Rendova Island on 30 June 1943, an American P-40 fighter with an external fuel tank flies overhead during the unopposed landing of the 172nd Infantry Regiment, US 43rd Infantry Division. The Curtiss P-40 'Tomahawk' (also called 'Warhawk' and 'Kittyhawk' by the British and Australians respectively) entered service in May 1940. It was reliable and powerful by 1930s standards and was an adequate fighter early in the war. Among the American Volunteer Group (AVG) in China ('Flying Tigers'), the P-40 was competitive against Japanese fighters. However, with the advent of the Japanese 'Zero' and 'Oscar' fighters, the P-40 evolved into a capable fighter-bomber for close support in all theatres. *(NARA)*

(**Opposite below**) An iconic photograph of American soldiers of the 172nd Infantry Regiment at the water's edge after landing at Rendova Point during a rain storm on 30 June 1943. The landing would place the Americans in close proximity to Munda Airfield across Blanche Channel on New Georgia Island proper. *(NARA)*

(**Above**) American infantry landing on Rendova Island on 30 June 1943 would face no more than 400 Japanese there. Nonetheless, many of the enemy would have to be ferreted out in the jungle. Here GIs begin the process of moving off the beach early on D-Day to enter the jungle to secure the island for the main mission – installation of heavy artillery to shell Munda Airfield. *(NARA)*

(**Opposite above**) American soldiers move through a Rendova coconut palm grove in a snaking single file to avoid bunching in the event of a Japanese mortar or grenade discharger ambush. Observing the post-invasion activity, Japanese General Sasaki began to order his garrisons in the eastern portion of the New Georgia group to withdraw through the jungle to Munda. (*NARA*)

(**Opposite below**) An American infantryman in tropical camouflage proceeds cautiously in a hunkered-down posture through the Rendova jungle with his M1 Garand rifle at the ready for any lurking Japanese snipers remaining on the island. The M1 Garand was the standard issue rifle of the US Army in the Second World War as well as being the first semi-automatic rifle to enter service with any of the combatant nations' armies. It was gas-operated and entered service to replace the Springfield Model 1903 bolt-action rifle that the Marines had used on Guadalcanal. (*NARA*)

(**Above**) An American infantryman aims his M1 Garand rifle at a Japanese sniper position in the Rendova jungle. The weapon fired a .30-06 inch cartridge that was fed by an 8-round en-bloc clip through an internal magazine. A skilled rifleman could fire 40–50 rounds per minute from this stable gun platform, with relatively low recoil, giving this weapon the distinction of the highest sustained rate of fire of any standard issue rifle during the war. It had an effective range of over 1,300 feet. However, it did have a considerable weight of 9.6lb unloaded as a disadvantage when trekking through the hot, humid jungles of the Solomon Islands and New Guinea. Another disadvantage was the distinctive noise that the loading clip made upon its ejection from the rifle after the eight rounds were expended, thus alerting the enemy of the shooter's location in dense jungle where visibility could be quite limited by the dense vegetation as shown. (*NARA*)

A dead Japanese soldier lies sprawled on the floor of the jungle of Rendova Island. His gas mask and other personal items lie off to the right of the corpse. As on Guadalcanal, Japanese defenders were tenacious and suicidal in their attempts to slow the advance of American infantry with limited resources. *(NARA)*

American infantrymen bring supplies from landing craft onto the beach after the unopposed successful assault on Rendova Island on 30 June 1943. Admiral Halsey wanted to accumulate sufficient material, ammunition and supplies by D-Day +4 to then mount his invasion of New Georgia proper, using Rendova as a stepping-stone as well as a huge artillery base to shell Munda Airfield. *(NARA)*

A group of American soldiers haul a 37mm anti-tank gun out of the surf and onto the beach at Rendova Point. Ammunition canisters in waterproof bags are suspended from the top of the gun's shield. Although nearly obsolete in other theatres by this time, the Marines on Guadalcanal had demonstrated the 37mm gun's effectiveness to break up Japanese infantry formations and frontal attacks when it fired canister rounds, essentially functioning as a giant shotgun. (NARA)

American soldiers manhandle 2.5-ton trucks laden with equipment from the shoreline onto the beach at Rendova Point. The transformation of Rendova from an amphibious assault site to a stepping-stone to the larger New Georgia Island was underway. However, the terrain would limit the speed of accomplishing this task. Since the volcanic soil of the Solomon Islands quickly turns to a thick, tenacious muck when rained upon, there were definitely no places that the landing force would refer to as dry land. (NARA)

(**Above**) Marines in camouflage uniforms form a human chain to unload supplies from Landing Craft Infantry (LCI) ships at Rendova Harbor shortly after securing the island in order to build up stockpiles of ammunitions and supplies for the upcoming attack on New Georgia. *(NARA)*

(**Opposite above**) US Navy Landing Ship Tanks (LSTs) with their bow ramps lowered at the shoreline are unloaded by soldiers on Rendova. Vehicles have probably been off-loaded already. Atop the vessels, wary sailors stand by their anti-aircraft guns to fire on low-flying enemy fighter sweeps if needed. *(NARA)*

(**Opposite below**) Five US Marines on Rendova attempt to pry out one of their Jeeps from the deep mud on the island using long wooden beams. It was quite common for trucks, Jeeps, and artillery pieces to become mired up to the tops of their wheel hubs in the tenacious, wet volcanic material. *(NARA)*

(**Above**) To facilitate vehicular movement through a deeply muddied path in a coconut palm grove, US Navy 'Seabees' lay out wooden logs across the mire to construct a corduroy road. These roads would be necessary to move supplies and artillery pieces into position for the New Georgia Island assault in early July 1943. (*NARA*)

(**Opposite above**) US Marines and Navy 'Seabees' carry a generator along a muddy trail that has been drying out. The apparent depth to a linear depression on the trail shows how deep a wheel from a vehicle sunk into the terrain. This crew of workers is walking past a 155mm 'Long Tom' cannon in the background. (*NARA*)

(**Opposite below**) A quartet of a members of a Marine 9th Defense Battalion man a .50-inch calibre anti-aircraft (AA) machine-gun mounted on a monopod with a pivoting top to fire at all angles against low-flying Japanese fighters that frequently strafed and bombed Rendova installations with anti-personnel bombs. First-hand accounts describe how enemy fighters would sweep in at tree-top level to hit their targets more accurately. However, the Japanese planes were also more vulnerable flying so low to machine-gunfire as attested by this group that had recently downed an IJN A6M Mitsubishi Reisen 'Zero'. (*NARA*)

(**Opposite above**) A Marine 9th Defense Battalion 40mm Bofors anti-aircraft (AA) gun-crew has its eyes trained skyward scanning for enemy fighters as US Navy Landing Craft Infantry (LCI) ships unload supplies, with Marines forming a human chain in the background while a Landing Craft Vehicle Personnel (LCVP), also called a 'Higgins boat', has its bow ramp down for unloading in the foreground. The Bofors was originally designed by the Swedish Navy, but all combatant nations manufactured this gun under license. Its relative ease of repositioning ashore and high rate of accurate fire proved devastating to enemy planes, as the majority of Japanese aircraft downed by surface ships or shore emplacements was achieved by this type of AA gun. (*NARA*)

(**Opposite below**) The crew of a 9th Marine Defense Battalion 155mm 'Long Tom' cannon rams a shell and powder charge into the breach of the weapon in preparation to fire on Munda Airfield across Blanche Channel from this coconut palm log embrasure on Rendova Point in early July 1943. (*NARA*)

(**Above**) A 9th Marine Defense Battalion 90mm anti-aircraft (AA) gun is pointed skywards behind its log and sandbag emplacement as the crew is prepared to load a shell in anticipation of a Japanese air attack on the Rendova installations. Australian coastwatchers on Bougainville or other Central Solomon Islands would sometimes be able to alert the defences on Rendova to prepare for an aerial assault. However, at other times the attack would be a surprise with planes flying in at tree-top level, as shown in the background. Bivouac tents are seen in the background to demonstrate the proximity that the crew lived to the AA gun due to the suddenness and ferocity of the Japanese fighter sweeps. Also, large cumulus clouds (background), or rain-filled early morning clouds, would shield the approaching Japanese aircraft. (*NARA*)

(**Above**) An aircraft-spotting-crew on a high point on the lookout for Japanese aircraft flying down over 'The Slot' to bomb and strafe the installations on Rendova. Like all the Solomon Islands, which arose from the ocean as volcano and mountain-studded terrain, Rendova was not flat. Rendova Mountain on the north-western side of the island, which overlooked the landing site and Munda Airfield across Blanche Channel, had a height of 3,448 feet. (*NARA*)

(**Opposite above**) After a Japanese air-raid, Navy Corpsmen drag a wounded Marine in camouflage uniform out from under the front of a truck that he hoped to use a cover from the enemy strafing and anti-personnel bomb blasts on the Rendova installations. (*NARA*)

(**Opposite below**) A wounded GI, victim of a concussion, lies face down in the mud after a recent Japanese air-raid. The Rendova beachhead, since it had large concentrations of men, equipment and supplies, made an excellent target for the Japanese pilots descending 'The Slot' from Rabaul. On 2 July, the Rabaul-based enemy planes killed at least thirty American servicemen, while wounding over 200 more. At night, roving Japanese destroyers would also shell the American installations on the island. (*NARA*)

Wounded American servicemen on Rendova are lifted by stretchers onto a Landing Craft Personnel (LCP) vessel to an awaiting Catalina Flying Boat (PBY) for air transport back to Guadalcanal for greater medical attention there. During a 2 July air-raid on the US beachhead at Rendova, in addition to the men and *matériel*, a 125-bed clearing-station staffed by the 118th Medical Battalion accompanying the 172nd Regimental Combat Team ashore with the landings was destroyed. As such, many of the wounded from the air-raids would be able to receive only emergency medical treatment, necessitating the air evacuation to Guadalcanal to receive full treatment. *(NARA)*

Three Marines from a 9th Marine Defense Battalion anti-aircraft (AA) gun-crew examine the wheel from a downed enemy bomber that washed ashore, among other salvage parts, on Rendova. So many Japanese planes were shot down in the vicinity of this AA position that it was nicknamed 'Suicide Point'. (NARA)

A Marine tractor hauls a 155mm 'Long Tom' cannon to a new position near Rendova Point to shell Munda Airfield. This fine artillery piece was one of the most important weapons in the South Pacific's long-range artillery inventory and, interestingly, was based on a French design used during the First World War. Over a decade had been required for this artillery piece, from design to implementation into service. The 'Long Tom' cannon's carriage with its ten wheels (eight on its gun-mount and two on the trail-mount) was specially designed to augment cross-country movement. (NARA)

Bibilo Hill

Kokengolo Hill

(**Opposite above**) Once hauled to a new firing position, the 'Long Tom' cannon's crew shifts it into position to fire on Munda Airfield. Next, an embrasure would need to be constructed to give the crew some protection against enemy counter-battery fire and aerial attack. At Munda Cape, the Japanese had half a dozen IJN 120mm and 140mm naval guns that had been used on D-Day to shell the American landing fleet. (*NARA*)

(**Above**) With its gun emplacement completed, a crew from A Battery of the Marine 9th Defense Battalion readies a shell for loading into their 155mm Long Tom cannon. They would fire their cannon over the tree-tops in the background and across Blanche Channel to Munda. The 'Long Tom' had a maximum range of over 25,000 yards and fired one 200lb round per minute. (*NARA*)

(**Opposite below**) Munda Airfield with Blanche Channel and Rendova Island (not seen) to the right. There are scattered Japanese aircraft near the revetments in this aerial reconnaissance photograph. Nearby, higher points are identified as Biblio Hill and Kokengolo Hill, the latter in the middle of the Munda complex from which Major Minoru (Noboru) Sasaki observed the Rendova landings on 30 June 1943. (*NARA*)

Japanese fighter planes lie destroyed on the ground. American artillery not only created large craters along the runway of Munda Airfield but inflicted extensive damage to planes that had not been evacuated to either Vila Airfield on Kolombangara Island or further north to airfields on or around Bougainville in the Northern Solomon Islands. (NARA)

Chapter Three

New Georgia Invasion and Assault on Munda (Operation *Toenails*)

In early May 1943, the commander of the Eighth Area Army on Rabaul, General Imamura, chose Major General Minoru (Noboru) Sasaki to lead the defence of New Georgia with the designation commanding general, South-east Area Detachment. Sasaki had three years of combat service, from 1939 to 1942, with an emphasis on mechanized warfare and on New Georgia, would be in command of troops of the 38th Infantry Group. Upon arriving on New Georgia, he demanded more men and supplies. With reinforcements, the Japanese garrison on New Georgia would number approximately 8,000 troops led by Sasaki, the finest field commander faced by Halsey's forces in the South Pacific.

Sasaki and his staff had inferred that the Americans would land on New Georgia and attempt an overland assault on Munda Airfield. This would enable Sasaki to get major reinforcements from southern Bougainville and Vila on Kolombangara so that he could construct a defence in depth at Munda. On 30 June, the Japanese observed that American soldiers from the 169th Infantry Regiment, in two-company strength, had occupied two islets, Baraulu and Sasavelle, on either side of Onaiavisi Entrance, the waterway leading from Blanche Channel into Roviana Lagoon and New Georgia's Zanana Beach, on the far side of the lagoon. This led General Sasaki to conclude that Zanana Beach was where Halsey intended to land on New Georgia in strength. Upon sighting the Americans on these islets astride Onaiavisi Entrance into Roviana Lagoon, Sasaki ordered his outlying garrisons in eastern New Georgia to withdraw to Munda.

After the successful landings at Rendova, Vice Admiral Halsey accelerated his timetable, having caught the Japanese off guard. He ordered US Army Major General John H. Hester, commander of the US 43rd Infantry Division (a New England National Guard Unit), now assigned as Commanding General New Georgia Occupation Force (NGOF), to move against Munda Airfield on New Georgia's Dragon Peninsula. This would be accomplished by Hester's command, on 3–5 July, initially ferrying troops over in landing-craft or coastal transport vessels (APCs) from

Rendova to New Georgia's Zanana Beach. His landing force would comprise major elements the 43rd Infantry Division's 169th and 172nd Infantry Regiments, a battalion of army field artillery, two battalions of Navy 'Seabees', a small detachment of the 1st Fiji Division, and elements of the 9th Marine Defence Battalion and the 4th Marine Raider Battalion from the Fleet Marine Force.

To assist isolating Munda Airfield, Marine Colonel Harry Liversedge was to take 2,600 Marines of only the 1st Raider Battalion of his 1st Marine Raider Regiment, (composed originally of the 1st and 4th Raider Battalions — however, the 4th Raider Battalion was deployed along the south coast of New Georgia), along with the 3rd Battalion from each of the 145th and 148th Infantry Regiments of the US 37th Division, on 4–5 July to occupy Rice Anchorage. This formation was designated the Northern Landing Force. Rice Anchorage was a swampy river delta east of the Japanese positions at Enogai Inlet and Bairoko Harbor. The Marines and soldiers, after arriving unopposed, were met with Japanese 140mm shelling from Bairoko Harbor, which scattered their naval landing force, leaving the Americans isolated and without supplies. Liversdege's force proceeded overland across Enogai Inlet on the north-west shore of New Georgia, opposite Kolombangara Island across Kula Gulf. The march to Enogai Inlet from Rice Anchorage was a protracted ordeal through flooded jungle swamps and rivers running high because of torrential rainfall. The approximately 8-mile overland march toward Bairoko Harbor took three days. The intent of this action was to prevent the Japanese from reinforcing the Munda area through Bairoko Harbor from the enemy base at Vila on Kolombangara Island. The mission to assault the Japanese garrison at Enogai Inlet was assigned to the 1st Raider Battalion, while the two 37th Division army battalions would be securing the inland trails and communication routes. After defeating the Japanese at Enogai Inlet by 10 July, at a cost of forty-five dead raiders and over a hundred other casualties, the remaining 1st Raider Battalion, along with the redeployed 4th Raider Battalion, the latter having landed at Enogai Inlet on 18 July, continued on to the main enemy position at Bairoko Harbor and assaulted in on 20 July. The raiders suffered grievously through a lack of air support and accurate Japanese heavy mortar fire necessitating their eventual withdrawal to Enogai Inlet. The Marines were dealt one of their few defeats in the South Pacific at Bairoko Harbor.

On 10 July, five days after the landings at Zanana Beach, General Hester's staff concluded that Sasaki's forces were dug into well-entrenched coral and log emplacements along the many hills leading to Munda. The NGOF would have to reduce these manned obstacles one at a time, often finding that others nearby were mutually supporting with an ample number of protected light and heavy machine-guns screened by infantry in nearby rifle pits. Japanese mortars as well as light artillery pieces and mountain guns were well-situated behind these defensive lines to wreak havoc on advancing American columns.

After receiving over 3,500 fresh Japanese infantry reinforcements from Kolombangara Island, General Sasaki deployed his 13th as well as the 229th Infantry Regiments along with elements of the 230th, the latter having fought on Guadalcanal. Added to the IJA forces were the 7th SNLF. Sasaki had previously interposed elements of the 13th Infantry Regiment between the American 169th and 172nd Infantry Regiments in the southern portion of New Georgia's Dragon Peninsula on 7 July. Now on 17 July, he would unleash his bold counter-attack against the American landing sites. However, poor communication, thick jungle and American defensive measures had severely impeded the enemy executing their counter-attack. Nonetheless, late on 17 July, the Japanese were able to turn the right flank of the American 43rd Division and were now situated on the Barike River poised for an attack against the Zanana beachhead supply area. The Japanese reached the American command post at Zanana beach, cutting the lines of communication to the 172nd Infantry Regiment to the south-west. American artillery on the offshore islands of Roviana and Sasavele in Roviana Lagoon, along with a valiant defence by Marine and 172nd Infantry Regiment heavy weapons platoons, hindered a concentration of Japanese forces to overrun the Zanana Beach. Fresh reinforcements would be needed and Major General Robert S. Beightler brought his 148th Infantry Regiment (less its 3rd Battalion that had landed at Rice Anchorage) to the battle.

Due to the extremely slow American advance, Vice Admiral Halsey sent in Lieutenant General Millard Harmon, South Pacific Ground Forces commander, to assess the situation. On 14 July, Harmon ordered Major General Oscar W. Griswold, commanding officer of US XIVth Corps (comprising both the 37th and 43rd Divisions), to take over the NGOF in mid-July, relieving Hester, who reverted back to command of the 43rd Infantry Division. Griswold had observed that the 43rd Division's 169th and 172nd Infantry Regiments were a spent force and unable to take Munda by themselves. He recommended that the 25th Division, along with the remaining battalions of the 37th Division, be deployed to resume the offensive effectively.

Utilizing Marine M3 light tanks and army infantry in support of the armour, progress was made during the last week of July as American forces moved on the Lambeti Plantation on the southern coast of the Dragon Peninsula in greater proximity to the Munda Airfield. Major General Robert Beightler and the remainder of his 37th Infantry Division had been previously deployed from Rendova on 7 July to participate in the gruelling march and struggle for Munda Airfield. In this action, Marine M3 light tanks of the 10th and 11th Defence Battalions would work alongside the army units that had become stalled on the jungle trails on the way to Munda. On 29 July, Major General Hodge replaced General Hester as commander of the 43rd Division, after a relatively poor showing by his 169th and 172nd Infantry Regiments. One week later, Munda Airfield was captured, which effectively surrounded the remaining tenacious Japanese defenders in the Munda area who had resorted to holing-up in caves in the Bibilo and Kokegolo Hills. On 5 August, XIVth Corps commander Griswold reported to Halsey that organized resistance in the Munda area had ceased and that many of the 30,000 American troops would now start mopping-up operations. Additionally, considerable effort would be required to repair the badly damaged Munda airstrip to make it operational again.

Elements of Major General J. Lawton Collins's 25th (Hawaiian) Division had been moving north-west since its landing at Zanana Beach on 21 July 1943. This division's trek took them through the jungle and swamp on the Munda-Bairoko trail. Collins's infantrymen were tasked with severing the supply route and path of retreat for any of the Japanese remaining on New Georgia who were not encircled in the Munda area. On 27 August, a battalion of Collins's 27th Infantry contacted patrols of Colonel Liversedge's combined Army and Marine Northern Landing Force. By the third week of August, both the 37th and 25th Division soldiers, along with elements of Liversedge's Northern Landing Force, entered Bairoko Harbor unopposed, an objective that eluded the Marines and soldiers from the 3rd Battalions of the 145th and 148th regiments on their 20–22 July assault. The major ground-fighting on New Georgia had ceased as General Sasaki had skilfully evacuated the remainder of his Bairoko garrison across Kula Gulf to Kolombangara on the night of 23 August in the wake of the fall of Munda Airfield to the Americans.

Arundel Island

To the north-west of New Georgia's Dragon Peninsula lies the relatively flat and heavily jungle-clad Central Solomon Islands of Arundel and Wana Wana (also referred to as Vona Vona). Both of these islands are directly south of Kolombangara with its Japanese airfield at Vila. General Sasaki wanted to use these islands as staging points to regain parts of western New Georgia following the loss of Munda Airfield and after receiving new reinforcements. However, on 6 August 1943, the 'Tokyo Express', laden with reinforcements from the Shortland Islands, was intercepted and the Japanese destroyer transports were sunk. General Sasaki would not receive any more reinforcements for New Georgia and he left the island for Kolombangara on 9 August. Nonetheless, Sasaki was under an IJN directive, dated 13 August, to hold out in the New Georgia group of islands for as long as he could to enable General Imamura to bolster the defences of the Northern Solomon Islands, especially Bougainville.

Elements of the American 37th Division, while attempting to clear parts of western New Georgia after the seizure of the Munda airfield, received artillery and small arms fire from Baanga and Arundel Islands, while members of the battle-scarred 43rd Infantry Division landed on Baanga Island on 10 August and secured it after ten days of combat, with the few Japanese survivors escaping to Arundel and Kolombangara Islands.

On 11 August, Halsey ordered Griswold to move into position on Arundel Island and shell Vila airfield on Kolombangara Island. Arundel is separated from the west coast of New Georgia by Hathorn Sound and Diamond Narrows. The 172nd Infantry Regiment invaded it unopposed on 27 August, except for a single company of the IJA 229th Regiment that harassed the invaders principally by sniping and nocturnal infiltration to sever lines of communication.

Then, the intensity of the enemy resistance was heightened due to Sasaki's orders to delay Halsey's forces for as long as possible. Sasaki, on 8 September, sent a battalion from his 13th Infantry Regiment, under Major Kikuda, from Kolombangara to strengthen his forces on Arundel Island. The American advance was retarded by a series of enemy-organized ambushes, so that Japanese artillery on Arundel Island could shell the newly acquired American airfield at Munda Point. The US 172nd Regiment's movement forward ceased two weeks after landing on Arundel Island, necessitating the deployment of elements of the US 27th, 169th and 103rd Infantry Regiments from the 25th, 43rd and 37th Divisions respectively, along with Marine tanks to secure it from fanatical Japanese resistance.

However, the Japanese on Arundel could not be resupplied due to US Navy interdiction in the waters of Kula Gulf and Blackett Strait. Without supplies due to American naval interdiction from Bougainville, Sasaki, still on Kolombangara, sent the remainder of his 13th Infantry Regiment on 14 September to Arundel Island with the forlorn plan to attack Munda via Arundel to capture foodstuffs. Eventually, Sasaki ordered his Arundel Island defenders back to Kolombangara, which ended the fighting on Arundel on 21 September. Sasaki had lost over 800 men on Arundel Island. However, the Japanese had held up the American advance for more than three weeks. This did, indeed, enable General Imamura and Vice Admiral Jinichi Kusaka, commander of the 11th Air Fleet at Rabaul, who was also in charge of all naval units in the Solomons, to bolster the defences of both Rabaul and Bougainville. American casualties on Arundel were approximately 300 men.

Vella Lavella

Originally, Halsey's plan called for the attack against Munda to be followed by the seizure of Vila airfield on Kolombangara, but the Japanese were correctly believed to be established on that island in considerable strength, with estimates of a garrison of just under 10,000 troops. Halsey did not want another protracted campaign to capture Vila, as he had at Munda. The American admiral stated:

> The undue length of the Munda operation and our casualties made me wary of another slugging match, but I didn't know how to avoid it.

Halsey and his staff had decided not to attack Kolombangara Island as a prelude to moving into the Northern Solomons and, instead, bypass the heavily defended island and prevent its resupply by naval and aerial interdiction.

The South Pacific Force would instead seize the lightly held island of Vella Lavella just under 15 miles to the north-west of Kolombangara. Intelligence estimates placed the Japanese garrison on Vella Lavella at roughly 1,000 troops. The admiral's staff reasoned that Vella Lavella, the northernmost island in the New Georgia group, could provide a forward air-base, once constructed, for future operations in the Northern Solomon Islands and could also geographically contribute to the severing of enemy supply to Kolombangara. On 15 August 1943, a Northern Landing and Occupation Force of over 6,500 troops, comprising the 25th Division's 35th Regimental Combat Team as the amphibious force, the 58th Naval Construction Battalion ('Seabees'), the 4th Marine Defence Battalion for anti-aircraft and beach defences, and the army's 25th Cavalry Reconnaissance Unit, landed unopposed at Barakoma, with the exception of some Japanese aerial attacks with bombers and fighters.

The Japanese realized that, in order to salvage the troops and equipment on nearby Kolombangara Island, they would need a nearby base, and Vella Lavella's northern tip seemed logical. To facilitate establishing a base there at Honaniu, two companies of the IJA 13th Infantry Regiment and some SNLF troops were landed there by armed barges on the night of 17–18 August.

Halsey noted that that the clearing of the Japanese on Vella Lavella was not moving according to plan. So he brought in reinforcements, comprising the 14th New Zealand Brigade of the 3rd New Zealand Division, which arrived on 18 September to complete the forcing of the enemy garrison into the north-west corner of the island occupation with a two-pronged offensive commencing 24 September. There was never any substantial ground combat on Vella Lavella because Japanese ground forces were both limited and in the process of withdrawing. However, the enemy did harass the 'Kiwis' advance through the jungles of Vella Lavella to stall Halsey's campaign in order to buy time to strengthen the Northern Solomon Islands. The sporadic fighting on Vella Lavella lasted until 5–6 October, as the Japanese employed tenacious delaying tactics. The real struggle for Vella Lavella occurred with naval surface action and incessant aerial attacks on American shipping, which included over a hundred enemy air attacks from 15 August to 3 September.

Halsey sent the navy's 'Seabees' to Vella Lavella to construct an airfield at Barakoma. The intent was to have fighters stationed there, which with auxiliary fuel tanks could reach Rabaul and make the return flight. The admiral also established a Marine staging base on Vella Lavella for future attacks in the Northern Solomons. To accomplish this, elements of the I Marine Amphibious Corps (IMAC) landed some units from the 3rd Marine Division at Ruravai further up Vella Lavella's eastern coast in mid-September.

On 20–21 September, as General Sasaki withdrew his Arundel Island forces, he also moved his troops off Gizo Island to Kolombangara Island, the latter of which would eventually have over 10,000 IJA and IJN troops. Two days later, the planning for the Kolombangara Island garrison's withdrawal began. It was Sasaki's responsibility to get these troops evacuated safely from a variety of Kolombangara Island's northern coastal points and bays. This was accomplished by offshore IJN destroyers receiving landing barges laden with Japanese troops from Kolombangara Island, commencing 28 September during a moonless night interval, and bringing those enemy ground-forces to the island of Choiseul, a six-hour direct northern sea voyage across 'The Slot'. By the end of the first week of October, the Kolombangara withdrawal was complete, despite attempts by US Navy surface vessels to interdict the evacuations. Those troops from Kolombangara that were not diverted to Choiseul were sent to either Bougainville or Rabaul. The evacuating Japanese troops from Vella Lavella were sent to the Shortland Islands off the southern coast of Bougainville. General Sasaki had managed to maintain the integrity of his forces during both the combat on and skilful evacuations from the islands of the New Georgia group in the Central Solomons. These Japanese forces would soon be able to fight Halsey's northern advance again.

Choiseul and the Treasury Islands

The Japanese suspected that Choiseul and the Shortland Islands would be Halsey's next target. On the night of 27–28 October 1943, Choiseul, south-east of Bougainville and north of Vella Lavella, was attacked by the 2nd Parachute Battalion of the 1st Marine Parachute Regiment, commanded by Lieutenant Colonel Victor H. 'Brute' Krulak, as a feint to confuse the Japanese about Halsey's real intention. Krulak's Marines continued their diversion until they were extracted on 4 November, by which time the Empress Augusta Bay invasion of Bougainville was already under way. Also, the Treasury Islands, lying directly south of both Bougainville and the Shortland Islands, would need to be occupied by Halsey's South Pacific Force to serve as advanced bases for small craft, including PT boats. The Treasurys were defended by only a few hundred Japanese and they were invaded by roughly 4,000 men of the 8th New Zealand Brigade Group on 27 October. However, the Allied commanders knew that the Japanese had about 25,000 troops stationed in the Buin-Shortland Islands area at the southern end of Bougainville, with the necessary barges to transport reinforcements to the Treasurys, so surprise and the coincident raid on Choiseul would be vital to keep the Japanese defenders confused as to where to commit their reserves. The Treasury Islands were successfully occupied by the Allies by the end of the first day's invasion with the small Japanese garrison being pushed into the jungle. By possessing the Treasury Islands, along with previously-occupied Vella Lavella, Halsey would have the advanced bases to support his Bougainville invasion and airfield construction, thereby avoiding the logistics crisis that he had on Guadalcanal where his base of supply was too remote at Noumea on New Caledonia. The first American planes landed at Vella Lavella on 24 September, thereby providing Halsey with another proximate airstrip to support his planned Cape Torokina beachhead, until a coastal fighter strip on Bougainville could be built by indispensable 'Seabees.' By mid-October, the American airfield on Vella Lavella would be accommodating approximately 100 aircraft.

The Japanese High Command in Tokyo remained puzzled by these Allied diversions, but the island assaults seemed to be producing the desired effect for Halsey's staff since Combined Fleet Commander Admiral Mineichi Kogo, who replaced the late Yamamoto, did not take any decisive action and remained highly suspicious of an immediate invasion of New Britain Island more so than Bougainville. According to Marine General Roy Geiger, who would take over the IMAC leadership from General Vandegrift on Bougainville on 9 November, the Treasury Island occupation and the Choiseul raid were important preliminary operations to landing on Bougainville's western coast serving as 'a series of short right jabs to throw the enemy off balance and to conceal the real power of our left hook to his belly at Empress Augusta Bay'.

A group photograph of several of the Australian coastwatchers. Lieutenant Commander Eric Feldt is in the middle row, fourth from the left. To Feldt's right is Lieutenant Commander Hugh MacKenzie. Corporal Frank Nash, in his US Army uniform, is seated in the bottom row on the far right. (*Author's Collection*)

Australian coastwatchers Major Donald G. Kennedy (*left*) and Lieutenant A.R. Evans (*right*) with US Marine Lieutenant William P. Coultas at Kennedy's compound on the Markham Plantation at Segi Harbor on New Georgia Island on 3 March 1943. In the background are some of Kennedy's armed natives who patrolled and guarded the coastwatcher's base. Coultas was a naval intelligence officer on Vice Admiral Halsey's staff. He had pre-war experience in the Solomon Islands and from that, he was able to converse with the natives in 'pidgin.' He was inserted into Segi Harbor by a Catalina flying boat (PBY), along with some Marine raider officers and enlisted men, to reconnoitre first-hand the area behind enemy lines that the Americans would soon invade as well as examine Kennedy's maps at his coastwatching base headquarters. Shortly after this photograph was taken, Evans would depart to Kolombangara Island to observe progress on the Japanese airfield being constructed there at Vila to support the enemy airdrome at Munda Point on the western part of New Georgia Island. (*AWM*)

Segi Point with its airfield on the south-eastern end of New Georgia is shown. A fighter strip was built there by the US Navy 'Seabees' to minimize the distance from airstrips on Guadalcanal and in the newly acquired Russell Islands. A Marine raider detachment was landed by US Navy destroyers at Segi Point on 20–21 June 1943, with orders to hold the area in the event of an anticipated large-scale Japanese assault, utilizing the entire Imperial Japanese Army (IJA) 1/229th Infantry Regiment, to seize Kennedy's compound. (*NARA*)

US Marine raider officers and war correspondents pose with some of Major Kennedy's armed native constabulary at his compound at Segi Point. The Marine raiders were sent to Segi Point to protect Kennedy's compound from an impending Japanese raid. As no major encounter occurred, this raider detachment, from the 4th Raider Battalion, would soon move overland to Viru Harbor, through intense rain and thick mud, to attack and seize the Japanese installation there. (NARA)

IJA Major General Noboru (Minoru) Sasaki, who was appointed to lead the defence of New Georgia with the designation commanding general, South-east Area Detachment, is shown. On New Georgia, Sasaki would be in command of troops of the 38th Infantry Group. From direct observations of the American landing on Rendova on 30 June 1943, Sasaki and his staff inferred that the Americans would land on New Georgia and attempt an overland assault on Munda Airfield. Sasaki mustered approximately 8,000 troops by recalling outlying garrisons and reinforcements from Bougainville and Kolombangara Island to construct a defence in depth at Munda as well as at Enogai Inlet and Bairoko Harbor north of the airfield. Halsey's staff regarded Sasaki as the finest Japanese field commander they faced in the South Pacific theatre. (NARA)

Marine raider Colonel Harry Liversedge at his field headquarters at Enogai Inlet after its capture on New Georgia Island. Liversedge was tasked to take 2,600 Marines of only the 1st Raider Battalion from his 1st Marine Raider Regiment, along with the 3rd Battalion from each of the non-seasoned 145th and 148th Infantry Regiments of the US 37th Division (an Ohio National Guard unit) on 4–5 July to occupy Rice Anchorage and then to march on Enogai Inlet and the well-defended IJN installation at Bairoko Harbor, where his force was to meet heavy opposition. Bairoko Harbor had to be seized to mitigate Japanese reinforcement of Munda from nearby Kolombangara Island. (USMC)

A Marine raider detachment crosses a malaria-infested jungle swamp on the way from Rice Anchorage to Enogai Inlet, which was just 2 miles from Bairoko Harbor. In addition to enemy attacks, the swollen waterways and thick mud from the torrential rains posed obstacles to the movement of Colonel Liversedge's troops. (NARA)

Marine raiders crouch amid the dense jungle vegetation on the way from Rice Anchorage to Enogai Inlet in early July 1943. The raiders had their march towards Enogai Inlet punctuated by attacks from IJA and SNLF infantry in company and larger strength. (*USMC*)

(**Opposite page**) Marine raider Private Roy Grier examines a Japanese SNLF officer's pistol after killing him in fighting around Bairoko Harbor. The Japanese officer died with a grenade in his hand as well. Grier's 0.45-inch calibre Thompson submachine-gun with a round drum magazine rests against his left leg. (*NARA*)

(**Below**) Exhausted Marine raiders muster the energy to display some of their battle trophies after having engaged strong Japanese forces at Enogai Inlet, which they captured after two days of combat. (*NARA*)

(**Above**) A Marine Scout Bomber Douglas (SBD) Dauntless dive-bomber patrols the waters around the Central Solomon Islands in preparation for an attack on New Georgia's Munda airfield. After air superiority was won following the Japanese defeat at Guadalcanal, the Dauntless was one the Pacific War's decisive aeroplanes, having already garnered the reputation of destroying four Japanese carriers at the Battle of Midway. It had a crew of two and could carry a 2,250lb bomb-load. It had a range of only just over 1,500 miles, so more proximate airfields, such as at Bougainville, would be required to bring these planes to bear to isolate Rabaul during Operation *Cartwheel*. (*NARA*)

(**Opposite page**) Plumes of smoke from American artillery fire billow from the area around Munda Airfield while a flight of Marine SBD Dauntless dive-bombers prepare to attack the runway. (*NARA*)

(**Below**) Marine SBD Dauntless dive-bombers from Henderson Field on Guadalcanal target the end of the runway at Munda Airfield during one of the many sorties to make the strip unusable by the enemy as combined Marine and Army troops advance through the jungle trails and Japanese defences to seize it. (*NARA*)

A Marine Defence Battalion 105mm Howitzer on New Georgia in maximal elevation fires a high-explosive shell at Munda Airfield, while another is readied for loading into the breech to neutralize both the enemy airstrip and surrounding defensive works that had been erected in depth to protect the site by Japanese Major General Sasaki. (*NARA*)

(**Opposite above**) In early August 1943, a column of M3 Stuart light tanks from one of the Marine Defence Battalions on New Georgia advances along a heavily wooded island trail to support army infantry units advancing on Japanese defences to get to Munda Airfield. As the Australians had effectively demonstrated at Buna in Papua, New Guinea in December 1942–January 1943, the tanks on New Georgia were also used as 'mobile pillboxes' to neutralize the extensive Japanese entrenchments that housed light artillery, machine-guns and riflemen. The main 37mm turret gun and machine-guns were brought to bear suppressive fire as well as armour-piercing rounds to penetrate the coral, logs and earth reinforcement to the enemy pillboxes. Despite the tanks' firepower, the relentless Japanese infantry still attacked the M3s with flamethrowers, grenades and magnetic mines, which disabled a few. Tactical cooperation between accompanying army infantrymen with the Marine armour proved vital to the success, albeit slow, in the advance on Munda. (*NARA*)

(**Opposite below**) After three days of nearly continuous combat in early August 1943, the Marine Defence Battalion crew members of an M3 Stuart light tank take a rest on their armoured vehicle. Two of the four tank crewmen are working on the 0.30-inch calibre Browning machine-guns that provided suppressive fire on the Japanese entrenched positions, thereby enabling infantry to get close enough to reduce the fortification with grenades, TNT satchels, or flamethrowers. The M3 Stuart light tanks were also used by the 3rd Marine Defence Battalion on Guadalcanal beginning in August 1942 to rout Japanese infantry and attack enemy fortifications during that island campaign. The effective use of Marine tanks in New Georgia's thick jungle and coconut groves would be aptly demonstrated. (*NARA*)

The graves of two Marine raiders from the 1st Raider Battalion are shown at a makeshift jungle cemetery on the trek to Enogai Inlet in July 1943. The mission of the raiders was to secure Enogai Inlet and Bairoko Harbor to prevent Japanese reinforcements of Munda from Kolombangara Island, but the price in Marine casualties was high. (*NARA*)

(**Opposite above**) A Marine raider honour guard from the 4th Raider Battalion of the 1st Raider Regiment fires a volley to salute their fallen comrades at Viru Harbor. The raiders, after not encountering any major enemy attack at Segi Point on the south eastern coast of New Georgia, marched overland through torrential rain and extremely muddy terrain to Viru Harbor to attack the Japanese installation there. After some fire-fights and a failed Japanese *banzai* charge by the roughly 250 men of the IJA 229th Infantry Regiment, the Marine raiders captured the enemy compound at Viru. After ferreting out snipers and some surviving Japanese in the New Georgia jungle, they turned over the area to army troops. The rest of the Japanese garrison took jungle trails back to Munda. By 1 July 1943, Viru Harbor with its naval shore-gun along with the garrison, ceased being an issue for the advancing American approach of General Hester's New Georgia Occupation Force. (*NARA*)

(**Opposite below**) Marines from the 1st Raider Battalion of the 1st Raider Regiment pay tribute to their recently buried comrades at a jungle cemetery site somewhere between Rice Anchorage and Bairoko Harbor. Intense fighting between Colonel Liversedge's raiders and IJA and SNLF infantry occurred in this extremely harsh terrain. (*NARA*)

Two Landing Craft Tanks (LCTs) are shown in the left background off Segi Point in the approach to New Georgia Island to bring army troops and supplies from Guadalcanal and the Russell Islands in the Southern Solomons for the continued assault on that Central Solomon Island by General Hester's New Georgia Occupation Force in mid-July 1943. The LCT was also capable of delivering bulldozers, medium tanks and heavy trucks ashore. Since the armaments on the LCTs were limited to one or two 20mm anti-aircraft cannon, more strongly armed, small 100-foot wooden coastal transport craft (APCs), as shown in the foreground provided excellent escort as well as being capable of transporting limited numbers of troops. (NARA)

Soldiers of the US 148th Infantry Regiment of the 37th Division in transit from Guadalcanal and the Russell Islands arrive on New Georgia Island on 22 July 1943. The 3rd Battalion from this regiment had previously been deployed with elements of the 1st Marine Raider Regiment to Rice Anchorage earlier in the month for the assaults on Enogai Inlet and Bairoko Harbor. These soldiers from the 148th Infantry Regiment, an Ohio National Guard Unit, would distinguish themselves fighting alongside the 43rd Infantry Division in the march on Munda Airfield, fighting the Japanese at locales such as Bartley Ridge and Horseshoe Hill, becoming surrounded at the latter from 26 July to 1 August 1943, until the Japanese evacuated their positions. (NARA)

Soldiers of the US 161st Infantry Regiment from the 25th (Hawaiian) Division descend along the walkways of a Landing Craft, Infantry (LCI) vessel on 22 July 1943. Just a year before, this regiment replaced the 298th Infantry Regiment in that division. This regiment and the remaining two of the 25th Division, the 35th and 27th, all saw action on Guadalcanal under Major General J. Lawton Collins. The disembarking soldiers of the 161st Infantry Regiment would soon reinforce the 37th Infantry Division, which had run into tenacious resistance by the Japanese as it started its assault on Munda Airfield. (*NARA*)

Soldiers of the US 172nd Infantry Division of the 43rd Division advance through a jungle creek with water up to their knees as they march towards Munda Airfield. This regiment had been stationed at Espiritu Island until March 1943 and then went to Guadalcanal. This regiment landed unopposed on Rendova Island on 30 June 1943 and then crossed over to New Georgia on 3–6 July. The 172nd Infantry, after its landing at Zanana Beach, marched to the south-west without much food or water, to arrive at Laiana on New Georgia's southern coast by 13 July, and with the aid of Marine Defence Battalion M3 light Stuart tanks was able to defend and expand its perimeter there in order to withstand a major enemy attack on 17 July by the 3rd Battalion of the IJA's 13th Infantry Regiment between Laiana and Zanana in the Sho River area, after it had been recently reinforced from Kolombangara Island a week earlier. Sasaki cabled Rabaul that it was time for the offensive to stop the American build-up and to destroy the beachheads at Laiana and Zanana. Laiana Beach, to the south-west, was 5,000 yards closer to Munda than Zanana, the original landing site. General Hester realized that, if he could secure a beachhead at Laiana, his supply lines to aid his 172nd and 169th Infantry Regiments would be considerably shortened. After landing at Zanana,

the 169th Regiment of the 43rd Division trekked due west across the more southerly portion of New Georgia's Dragon Peninsula, which placed them to the north of their sister regiment, the 172nd. However, since the 169th had fallen behind in its march, the northern flank of the 172nd would be open to Japanese infiltration that would threaten their lines of communication and supply. (*NARA*)

(**Opposite above**) American soldiers of the 27th Infantry Regiment, 25th Division carefully look for snipers on their difficult jungle march through creeks and swamps in order to reach the Piru Plantation prior to taking Zieta, on New Georgia's west coast to the north of Munda, on 15 August 1943. The 25th Division, after landing at Zanana, would traverse the more northerly sector of New Georgia's Dragon Peninsula. After Zieta's seizure, the 27th, along with the 37th Division's 145th Infantry Regiment, occupied Bairoko Harbor on 25 August 1943 and then participated in mopping-up operations until the entire island was deemed secure by 15 September 1943. (*Author's Collection*)

(**Opposite below**) American soldiers patrol near enemy positions by carefully fording a creek with chest-high water, as can be seen in the left background, while GIs stand guard with their rifles ready for an ambush in the foreground. In addition to the waterways and tenuous crossings, malaria, mud, jungle and enemy air sorties sapped the energy of both the 169th and 172nd Infantry Regiments of the 43rd Division. (*NARA*)

Two GIs crouch down in a foxhole serving as a forward observation post along a trail with a tent half-sheet serving as a protective roof from the incessant rain in the New Georgia jungle in July 1943. The soldier on the left holds his M1918 Browning automatic rifle (BAR) while the one on the right cradles the now army standard-issue M1 Garand semi-automatic rifle. The BAR was originally designed during the First World War and first used by the US Army in September 1918. It was very heavy, at 22lb (loaded), for its limited trapezoidal magazine capacity of twenty .30-inch calibre rounds. Although the firing rate ranged from 350 to 550 rounds per minute, in practice, because of the frequent magazine changes, it was only sixty to eighty rounds per minute. The gas-operated M1 Garand entered service in 1936, replacing the Springfield Model 1903 bolt-action rifle. However, it was not widely distributed to soldiers until 1940. The Marines, too, had adopted the Garand in 1940. However, supplies of the produced weapons went to the Army on a prioritized basis. (NARA)

Soldiers of the 148th Infantry Regiment of the 37th Division carry hot food in washed-out gasoline cans to the front lines. The 1st and 2nd Battalions of the 148th were brought to New Georgia from Guadalcanal and the Russell Islands during the third week of July to reinforce the faltering 169th and 172nd Infantry Regiments of the 43rd Division moving west from Zanana Beach towards Munda. (NARA)

A Marine Landing Vehicle, Tracked (LVT) moves along a muddy path in front of a Jeep as it passes American soldiers with full kit resting nearby. The LVT was designed in the United States for use in the Florida swamps. These amphibians were widely used in the South Pacific from Guadalcanal onwards to perform a multitude of tasks in and out of combat. The LVTs had a variety of armaments, including .50-inch calibre machine-guns, 20mm Polsen cannon, and even flame-throwers. (NARA)

Troops of the 37th Division carry ammunition to the front line via a jungle trail. Dense woods are on either side of the passageway and could always harbour a Japanese ambush site or snipers. (*Author's Collection*)

A US Army veteran on New Georgia exhibits the prototypical forward-gazing stare of a soldier who has recently seen protracted combat. He sits with his rifle slung over his shoulder and is about to eat a can of his rations. (*USAMHI*)

A US Army 43rd Infantry Division patrol searches for a Japanese dugout in the thick New Georgia jungle on 9 July 1943, just days after landing on the island. Here, a GI swings across a stream on a jungle vine as one of his patrol mates prepares to catch him. The other patrol members in the background have their eyes trained on the jungle, wary of enemy snipers. (*USAMHI*)

A US soldier with his M1 Garand at the ready covers the return of his platoon mates from a mission to destroy an enemy machine-gun nest along a jungle trail on the way to Munda in July 1943. The patrol is descending a creek's embankment and is using a log across the waterway to support their footing. (*NARA*)

(**Above left**) Two GIs dart through dense jungle vegetation to ferret out enemy positions along the Munda Trail. Safe distances had to be kept between soldiers to minimize casualties from Japanese mortar rounds and the enemy's grenade dischargers. (*NARA*)

(**Above right**) A Japanese mortar round explodes in the background with its visible plume of smoke as two American soldiers warily proceed forward. As is evident, visibility was often limited to a few yards ahead, while the vegetation and enemy's camouflage could perfectly conceal an ambush site. (*NARA*)

(**Opposite page**) An American soldier lies prone and fires his M1 Garand rifle on the lip of an enemy dugout in the background. In the foreground, a Japanese soldier who had occupied the sniper hole lies dead. As on Guadalcanal, the Japanese resistance to the American advance on Munda was suicidal. (*NARA*)

US Army Corporal John Rothschild (*left*) gives report to his company captain about how he and his machine-gun assistant, Private Wantuck, both of a 172nd Infantry Regiment heavy weapons platoon, had sighted a light machine-gun to fire down a trail on which hundreds of Japanese infantrymen were approaching Zanana on the night of 17 July 1943. Scores of Japanese were killed by machine-gun fire and ensuing hand-to-hand combat, which claimed Private Wantuck's life. Both Wantuck and Rothschild received Navy Crosses for their heroism in preventing the Zanana beachhead from being overrun, which would have severely interrupted the American supply route into New Georgia. (*NARA*)

(**Opposite above**) In close proximity to the Munda Airfield, with Blanche Channel in the background, an army flame-thrower unit sends a plume of flame at a Japanese pillbox protecting the airstrip. To support the flame-thrower, two soldiers provide suppressive fire against the pillbox and any associated enemy infantry in a rifle pit. (*NARA*)

(**Opposite below**) An American soldier talks via a telephone line to a crew member of a Marine Defence Battalion M3 light tank during the advance towards Munda in late July 1943. The close interaction between army infantry and Marine tanks became necessary when it was apparent that the armour was proving to be most effective in spear-heading jungle assaults against Japanese entrenchments, because they were relatively impervious to enemy small arms fire and the 37mm turret gun could directly reduce many of the hidden coral and log-reinforced bunkers, some of which housed enemy anti-tank guns. However, the Marine armour could not safely function unless they had infantry support with flame-throwers, soldiers with hand-grenades and personal weapons to be used against lurking enemy infantry who would try to destroy the tanks in a rush with anti-tank mines and grenades. Australian-crewed M3 light tanks had previously been proven to be vital to reduce Japanese fortifications in Giropa Plantation in order to capture Buna in Papua, New Guinea in late December 1942–early January 1943. (*NARA*)

(**Above**) Major General Robert S. Beightler (*left*), commanding general of the US 37th Division and Ohio National Guard Unit, sits at an impromptu field conference with some of his officers at the front on New Georgia in late July 1943. One battalion of his 148th Infantry Regiment had been sent to Rice Anchorage in early July to fight along with elements of the 1st Marine Raider Regiment, while the other battalions of this regiment were added to the combat on New Georgia from 18–22 July on orders by US XIVth Corps commander Griswold to relieve the 43rd Division's 172nd Regiment. Two battalions of the 37th Division's 145th Infantry Regiment would relieve the 43rd Division's 169th Regiment. Both elements of the 145th and 148th Regiments disembarked from Guadalcanal and the Russell Islands in mid-to-late July 1943. (*NARA*)

(**Opposite above**) Major General J. Lawton Collins (*right*), commanding general of the 25th Division, sits in the jungle and confers with one of his subordinates. Elements of the 25th Division were proceeding north-west after landing at Zanana on 21 July to link up with Colonel Liversedge's Northern Landing Force to effect another assault on Bairoko Harbor, as well as interdicting any Japanese supply trails or an escape route to and from the Munda area. (*NARA*)

(**Opposite below**) An American soldier, with his M1911 A1 semi-automatic 0.45-inch pistol, carefully surveys the opening to the rear entrance of a Japanese pillbox at Munda Airfield. It was through this rear portal to the entrenchment that the Japanese could covertly resupply and reinforce the position from mutually supporting sites in the immediate vicinity, while the aperture housing either a machine-gun or anti-tank weapon was extremely well-concealed and almost invisible to the advancing American infantry with or without accompanying Marine M3 light tanks. (*NARA*)

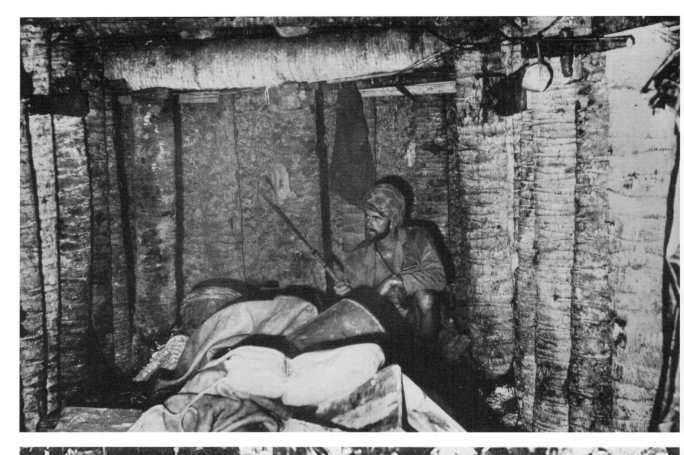

Two walking wounded GIs cross some rocky terrain as they help each other back to a rear echelon aid station. The soldiers still carry their personal weapons with the one on the left holding his 0.45-inch calibre Thompson submachine-gun with a drum magazine, while the GI on the right has his M1 Garand slung over his left shoulder. The Allies had learned at great cost in military personnel and negative morale after the debacles of both the British retreat in Burma in 1942 and Wingate's Operation *Longcloth* in 1943 that simply leaving the wounded (and accompanying medical caregivers) with either local villagers or to the Japanese resulted in executions and atrocities and was no longer an option. Additionally, disease-laden mosquitoes, poisonous scorpions, biting flies and leeches were infesting the impenetrable forests and swamps, which often constituted the hellacious combat locales of the South Pacific islands. *(NARA)*

(**Opposite above**) A Marine examines equipment left behind in a probable enemy bomb shelter or entrenched unit headquarters position, as suggested by equipment items attached to the coconut log beams. As is evident, this log-reinforced entrenchment would probably require a direct aerial bomb or a heavy calibre artillery shell to reduce it had the Japanese not abandoned this position on the orders of General Sasaki in the waning days of the campaign to seize Munda Airfield during the first week of August 1943. *(NARA)*

(**Opposite below**) A casualty of jungle fighting on New Georgia is carried out of thick vegetation on a stretcher to be placed onto a Jeep modified into an ambulance for transport to a rear echelon aid station. Often routes through the jungle-laden battlefields of the South Pacific Islands were no wider than a column of troops trekking in single file. Since the combat front was literally yards away, a four-man litter team was usually accompanied by one or two infantrymen with Thompson submachine-guns, which were well-suited for close combat defence in the jungle. Within minutes of someone getting hit and after being initially treated and assessed by a company combat medic, the wounded soldier would have field dressings and tourniquets applied to stop the bleeding, and by placement of an antibiotic, sulphonamide powder onto the wound, an initial attempt to minimize the likelihood of infection would be made. At this initial juncture of treatment in the jungle, medics learned that dressings had to be dyed khaki or green, because Japanese snipers took aim at white bandages. Even casualties, at times, tore off their white bandages in order to prevent becoming an easy target. *(NARA)*

(**Above**) Wounded soldiers lie on rows of litters aboard a lighter offshore of Munda in the process of being transported for additional care. Soldiers in the Pacific usually fared worse than their counterparts in Europe. An actuarial approach was even taken to assign the chance of survival after being seriously wounded. If appropriate and adequate treatment were initiated within an hour, there was a 90 per cent chance of recovery, whereas after eight hours the likelihood for survival was 25 per cent. Thus, the more rapid movement of the wounded to advanced field hospitals increased the survival chances of battlefield casualties considerably. Medical personnel preferred air to sea, since evacuation by ship entailed many transfers of the wounded from ambulance to lighter, and from lighter to ocean craft. However, the vast ocean distances in the South Pacific limited air transport evacuation of casualties to either PBY Catalina Flying Boats or C-47 transports from islands with suitable airfields. (*Author's Collection*)

(**Opposite page**) A Japanese field marker is inspected by an American soldier at Munda Airfield after the strip's capture in early August 1943. The enemy defences in the Munda area had to be reduced one at a time, often by combined infantry-tank cooperative tactics. The American westward advance towards the airstrip in the last days of July 1943 could be measured between 500 to 1,200 yards per day. Not only were the Japanese extremely tenacious in their fortified positions, but the swampy terrain also hindered the American advance. (*NARA*)

(**Above**) American road rollers in the middle and to the right help smooth the airfield surface after months of shelling and bombing. A captured Japanese road roller is off to the far left. The shoreline vegetation around the Munda Airfield has been devastated by American gunfire and bombing. (*NARA*)

(**Opposite above**) A Marine Vought F4U-1 Corsair takes off from battle-scarred Munda Airfield. The Corsair, with its inverted-gull wing design, was planned as a carrieborne fighter for the US Navy. However, as both carrier environment problems and ground combat success would soon demonstrate, it became an excellent ground-attack and close-support fighter, which fulfilled Marine aviation philosophy to lend assistance to the Corps' rifle platoons on the ground reach their objective with a minimum of casualties. The Corsair entered operational service in 1943. The aircraft was armed with external bombs or a rocket load of 2,000lb to complement the six 0.50-inch calibre forward-firing machine-guns in the leading edges of the wings. (*NARA*)

(**Opposite below**) US Navy and Marine Corps Grumman TBF-1 'Avengers' are lined up on Munda Airfield in September 1943 after the airstrip was resurfaced and Japanese resistance ceased. After making a disastrous combat debut at Midway in June 1942, where entire squadrons were destroyed by Japanese naval anti-aircraft gunfire and fighters, the TBF 'Avenger' rapidly matured as the classic torpedo bomber of the South Pacific war. The TBF-1 'Avengers' would participate in Halsey's carrier attack by the *Saratoga* and *Princeton* on Rabaul's Simpson Harbor on 5 November 1943, days after the Bougainville invasion at Cape Torokina. This aircraft was rugged and could take punishment from Japanese fighters, enabling them to return to their flight decks or airfields with extensive battle damage. The one 0.50-inch calibre Browning rearward-firing trainable machine-gun in the dorsal turret along with a 0.30-inch calibre rearward-firing machine-gun in the ventral position gave this aircraft some needed defensive firepower from trailing Japanese 'Zero' and 'Oscar' fighters. (*NARA*)

American soldiers of the 172nd Infantry Regiment of the battle-weary 43rd Division advance in thick brush in pursuit of retreating Japanese troops on Arundel Island, to the west of New Georgia across Hathorn Sound and the Diamond Narrows. Although in retreat, the Japanese were still offering stout defence against the American advance in compliance of an IJN directive of mid-August 1943 to retard Halsey's northward movement for as long as possible to enable a build-up of enemy forces in the Northern Solomons. (*NARA*)

Three soldiers of the 172nd Infantry Regiment crouch down in Arundel Island's dense vegetation from Japanese sniper fire while a tank moves through the jungle. The Japanese also managed to get 47mm anti-tank guns deployed against the Marine M3 light tanks, some of which were destroyed by enemy fire. (*NARA*)

In addition to the Marine and army artillery units pounding Vila Airfield on Kolombangara Island from both Arundel Island and western New Georgia, across Hathorn Sound, the 4.2-inch chemical mortar was to make its South Pacific combat debut on Arundel Island. By adding more discs to this weapon's barrel, a shell could be hurled up to a maximum range of almost 4,400 yards. (*NARA*)

A Marine 155mm Howitzer under a camouflage net on Arundel Island fires a round across Blackett Strait and the Kula Gulf at Vila Airfield on the south-eastern tip of Kolombangara Island. The Marines in this Defence Battalion Howitzer crew are wearing no more than their undershorts or fatigue trousers. (*NARA*)

(**Opposite above**) From 28 September to 7 October 1943, the mass evacuation of Japanese forces on Kolombangara Island was conducted. Halsey's strategy to bypass Kolombangara Island had been a success. The South Pacific Force had acquired the Vila Airfield on the island's south-eastern tip and unlike Munda Airfield there would be no amphibious invasion with its attendant supply problems or vicious combat against Sasaki's roughly 10,000 well-entrenched troops. An example of such a camouflaged, entrenched 20mm twin pom-pom anti-aircraft position at Vila Airfield is shown. (*NARA*)

(**Opposite below**) A Japanese steamroller captured during the American occupation of Vila Airfield after General Sasaki's evacuation of Kolombangara Island, from 28 September to 7 October 1943 is shown. (*NARA*)

(**Opposite above**) Two American soldiers stand at the rear entrance to an extremely well-camouflaged Japanese pillbox at Vila Airfield after Kolombangara Island's unopposed occupation in October 1943. The extensive array of palm fronds would have concealed this position until American infantry or tanks were fired on by the machine-guns or light artillery in the coral and log-fortified structure. (*NARA*)

(**Above**) A vertical marker to a non-battle-scarred Japanese cemetery near Vila Airfield on Kolombangara Island. The Japanese tried to retrieve the ashes of their fallen comrades and bring them back. However, General Sasaki's first priority was to supervise the logistics that were stretched to get the 10,000 IJA and IJN troops off Kolombangara Island with armed landing barges from the island's northern coast to offshore waiting destroyers. (*NARA*)

(**Opposite below**) A Japanese fighter lies wrecked near Vila Airfield on Kolombangara Island after the American capture followed the Japanese evacuation of the island. Extensive artillery and 4.2-inch chemical mortar-fire from Arundel and New Georgia Islands made Vila inoperable for Japanese aircraft late in the Central Solomons campaign, which commenced in late June 1943. (*NARA*)

(**Above**) A captured Japanese 20mm anti-aircraft gun in a weapons emplacement near Vila Airfield is shown. Halsey's staff did not want to wage combat against the 10,000 Japanese defenders of Kolombangara Island. Therefore, he bypassed it and headed north-westward to Vella Lavella. Halsey's decision not to attack Kolombangara Island and seize Vila Airfield was especially influenced by the thirty-five days of combat on New Georgia to seize Munda Airfield. The New Georgia Island invasion ultimately required 50,000 American troops, which was over three times the amount allocated in the original plan for Operation *Toenails,* to overcome the anticipated 9,000 Japanese defenders on New Georgia. American losses to capture New Georgia with the vital Munda Airfield were 1,000 dead and over 4,000 wounded. Halsey wanted no repeat of that to acquire Vila Airfield. (*NARA*)

(**Opposite above**) American soldiers from the US 25th Infantry Division clamber over the sides of a Landing Craft, Personnel (LCP) on 15 August 1943 onto the shoreline of the southern end of Vella Lavella near Barakoma. The island of Vella Lavella, just to the north-west of Kolombangara Island, was originally defended by only 250 survivors from Munda along with some marooned Japanese sailors following the sinking of their surface ships to US Navy gunfire and aerial attacks. This move by Halsey's staff effectively outflanked General Sasaki and his extensive garrison on Kolombangara Island. The Japanese were stunned as they had prepared Kolombangara Island for combat and as a major delaying action to retard the advance of Halsey's South Pacific Force. It had not occurred to the Japanese leaders on Rabaul that Halsey might bypass Kolombangara Island. As there was never any plan to launch a major offensive to stop the American landings at Vella Lavella, only small numbers of additional Japanese reinforcements were sent to Vella Lavella to bring the enemy strength to about 1,000 men. (*NARA*)

Infantrymen from the 25th Division's 35th Regimental Combat Team (RCT), roughly 4,600 troops, landed on Vella Lavella's south-eastern tip at Barakoma Beach on 15 August 1943. Here, a pair of GIs wait in thick jungle vegetation for the order to move northward from Barakoma. The soldiers to the left and in the centre are holding their M1 Garand semi-automatic rifles. (USAMHI)

(**Above**) Infantrymen from the 14th Brigade of the 3rd New Zealand Division landed on the north-west and north-east coasts of Vella Lavella on 25 September 1943 to relieve the American troops there as well as drive the remaining Japanese, using delaying tactics, into a pocket on the island's north-west coast. Many of the New Zealanders are wearing their distinctive 'lemon-squeezer' slouch hats, which had pointed crowns indented on every quarter. The brim of the slouch hat was narrower than the Australian version and was never folded up. The Japanese, as on New Georgia, were well-entrenched, which limited the 'Kiwi' advance under Major General H.J.E. Barrow-clough to 200–600 yards per day. Nonetheless, both Japanese and Allied casualties were light and the enemy withdrew in landing barges from their island's north-west pocket of resistance on the night of 8–9 October (*NARA*)

(**Opposite above**) Although the ground combat on Vella Lavella was limited, Japanese aerial attacks and naval surface ship engagements were extensive and really comprised the battle for this Central Solomon Island. Here a US Navy destroyer fires at enemy barges and destroyers as they attempt evacuation of General Sasaki's 10,000-man garrison from Kolombangara Island in stages. (*NARA*)

(**Opposite below**) New Zealand troops unload supplies from their assault boats after occupying the Treasury Islands south of Bougainville, on 27 October 1943, in order to distract the Japanese commanders' attention away from the upcoming main amphibious operation on Cape Torokina in Empress Augusta Bay on 1 November. Also, as a diversion on the night of 28 October, the 2nd Marine Parachute Battalion was inserted onto Choiseul, a large Northern Solomon island to Bougainville's south-east. To lend authenticity to this feint by Halsey's planners, the Marines tied down Japanese forces on Choiseul's northern half for seven days, with extraction of the force on 4 November. With Allied threats to the south and south-east of Bougainville prior to Halsey's invasion at Empress Augusta Bay, the Japanese reallocated their defences against these threats accordingly and neglected reinforcing the western side of the island at Cape Torokina. (*NARA*)

Lieutenant Colonel Victor H. Krulak, who led the 2nd Marine Parachute Battalion during the Choiseul raid on 28 October– 4 November 1943. His Navy Cross and Purple Heart citations for his gallantry on Choiseul reads in part: 'Assigned the task of diverting hostile attention from the movements of our main attack force *en route* to Empress Augusta Bay, Bougainville Island, Lieutenant Colonel Krulak landed at Choiseul and daringly directed the attack of his battalion against the Japanese, destroying hundreds of tons of supplies and burning camps and landing barges. Although wounded during the assault on 30 October he repeatedly refused to relinquish his command and with dauntless courage and tenacious devotion to duty, continued to lead his battalion against the numerically superior Japanese forces'. (*USMC*)

Chapter Four

Bougainville Invasion at Empress Augusta Bay (Operation *Cherry Blossom*) and Beachhead Expansion

American tactical planning for the Bougainville assault began in July 1943 when Halsey assigned the invasion's ground forces command, I Marine Amphibious Corps (IMAC) Headquarters, to Marine Lieutenant General Alexander Vandergrift after the unexpected and controversial death of Marine Major General Charles Barrett. MacArthur wanted Halsey's aircraft established within fighter range of Rabaul in time to assist with the neutralization of that major Japanese base as well as to cover the SWPA's invasion of Cape Gloucester on the southern end of New Britain, which was planned for between 25 December 1943 and 1 January 1944. Thus, MacArthur deemed it strategically necessary for Halsey's South Pacific forces to establish themselves on the mainland of Bougainville on 1 November 1943.

MacArthur placed the tactical location for Bougainville's invasion squarely in Halsey's hands. The Americans had the bitter realization that the IJA forces on Bougainville were far more formidable than they appeared on either Guadalcanal or New Georgia, and this produced a change in Halsey's plans for the move northward, even as the fighting was continuing at Munda, in the Dragon Peninsula, and on the surrounding islands in the Central Solomons.

Halsey and his South Pacific Force staff's strategic outlook and tactical planning had to evolve in order to establish a beachhead on Bougainville without a repetition of a bloodbath. The New Georgia campaign had claimed over 1,000 dead and nearly 4,000 wounded from the major elements of the three army divisions and Marine raider units ultimately thrown into combat for that Central Solomon island. Largely due to the combat exhaustion of the 25th and 43rd Infantry Divisions on New Georgia, and the commitment of the 1st Marine and 2nd Marine Divisions to MacArthur's Cape Gloucester assault and Admiral Nimitz's Central Pacific Islands offensive respectively, Halsey's South Pacific Force was left with only the unbloodied

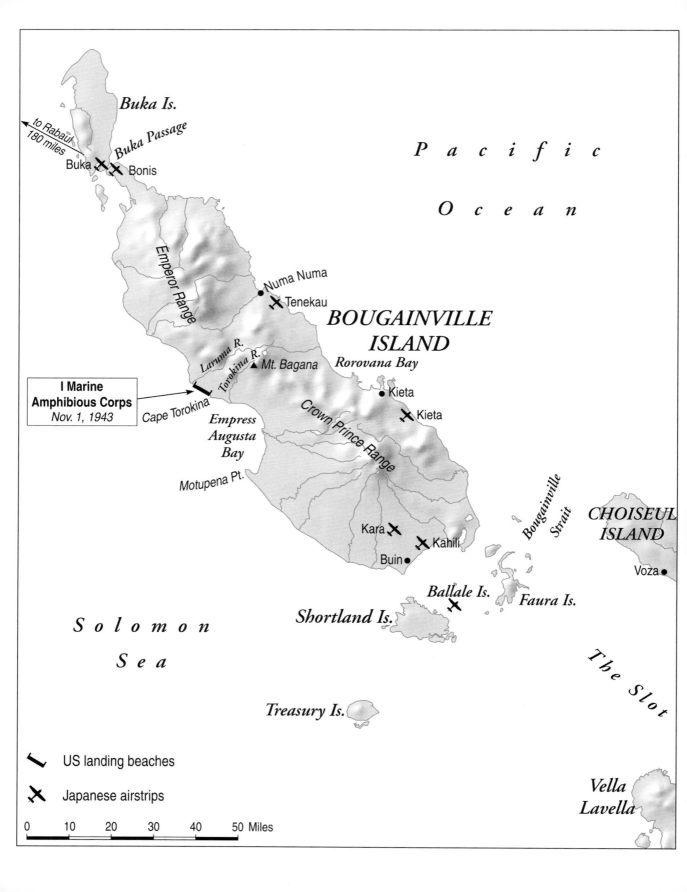

Buka Is.

to Rabaul 180 miles

Buka Passage

Buka ✕✕ Bonis

P a c i f i c

O c e a n

Emperor Range

● Numa Numa

✕ Tenekau

BOUGAINVILLE ISLAND

Laruma R.

Torokina R.

▲ Mt. Bagana

Rorovana Bay

● Kieta

✕ Kieta

I Marine Amphibious Corps *Nov. 1, 1943*

Cape Torokina

Empress Augusta Bay

Crown Prince Range

Motupena Pt.

Kara ✕

✕ Kahili

Buin ●

Bougainville Strait

CHOISEUL ISLAND

Voza ●

Ballale Is.

Faura Is.

Shortland Is.

S o l o m o n

S e a

The Slot

Treasury Is.

Vella Lavella

╲ US landing beaches

✕ Japanese airstrips

0   10   20   30   40   50 Miles

3rd Marine Division and the army's 37th Infantry Division, the latter having seen extensive action on New Georgia, for the initial phase of the Bougainville venture.

For Halsey, a less-daring strategic coup was going to be necessary to capture and construct new airfields on Bougainville, in order to utilize that island's proximity to Rabaul for an aerial assault on that Japanese bastion. Operation *Cartwheel* was to involve heavy bombers from air-bases in the Southern Solomons and New Guinea, supplemented by medium Navy and Marine dive and torpedo bombers to attack Rabaul from newly built airfields on Bougainville. A bloody assault on strong enemy formations and airdromes, such as in the Shortland Islands, off Bougainville's southern coast, or aimed at Buin itself on southern Bougainville, that was certain to make the front pages of stateside newspapers due to anticipated high casualty figures, was not an option.

The loss of New Georgia and the bypassing of Kolombangara somehow produced a reversal of the defeatism mindset that the Japanese suffered from after the loss of Guadalcanal and Papua during the early winter months of 1943. On 30 September 1943, Imperial Headquarters had instructed local Japanese commanders to hold the south-eastern front for as long as possible. Orders came from Tokyo that indicated Rabaul had to remain the centre of this defence line. Major efforts were made to repel the Allies by a tenacious defence at Bougainville in the Northern Solomon Islands and in North-eastern New Guinea. Bougainville had been built up as a major base by Admiral Yamamoto several months earlier. Now Bougainville was to become

Map 3. Bougainville and surrounding islands in the Northern Solomons are shown. Bougainville is one of the most northern in the Solomon Island chain as well as the largest, being 130 miles in length and 30 miles in width. In early October 1943, the Japanese had approximately 37,000 troops on Bougainville and nearby islands. Vice Admiral Halsey had targeted Cape Torokina in Empress Augusta Bay as his invasion site by the I Marine Amphibious Corps (IMAC) on 1 November, despite its proximity to Japanese airfields at Kahili and Kara, 65 miles to the south on Bougainville and Rabaul's airdromes 215 miles to the north-west. Other Japanese airfields on Bougainville were at Tenekau and Kieta to the north-east and Bonis to the north-west of Cape Torokina. Buka Island, just north of Bougainville, possessed an airfield, as did Ballale Island to the south. Halsey and his staff had calculated that the anticipated small Japanese garrison at Cape Torokina would justify the risk of the landing beaches' heavy surf there. He further surmised that the imposing Emperor and Crown Prince Mountain Ranges surrounding Empress Augusta Bay's coastal plain would delay a Japanese counter-attack by the bulk of the island's large garrison with artillery for at least several months. Halsey's South Pacific Force also conducted some small amphibious operations to keep the Japanese defenders off balance, thereby immobilizing some of their large troop dispositions that included 25,000 soldiers in southern Bougainville and the Shortland Islands, 5,000 on the east coast, and 5,000 at the island's northern end and on Buka Island. On 27 October, Choiseul, to the south-east of Bougainville, was attacked by the 2nd Marine Parachute Battalion as a feint to distract Japanese attention from Halsey's real amphibious invasion at Cape Torokina. The Marine Parachutists harassed the Japanese on the northern part of Choiseul for seven days before withdrawing. Also on 27 October, New Zealand and American troops captured the Treasury Islands south of Bougainville and the Shortland Islands as another diversion. The Japanese commanders thus perceived threats everywhere, except at Cape Torokina to the west and concentrated their defences away from the intended IMAC assault beaches. (Philip Schwartzberg, Meridian Mapping)

the staging area for renewed Japanese aerial attacks to the south and east, since it accumulated both military material and had a plethora of air force installations. Imbued with the spirit of *bushido,* the combination of tenacious Japanese resistance on Bougainville and its surrounding waters, along with an offensive air campaign against the Southern Solomons, was to give the leaders in Tokyo the necessary time for the IJA to supply and execute two land offensives in China and through Burma's western boundary into India. Victories in these operations might do irreparable harm to and derail Allied war plans in the Pacific theatre.

As the troops from Kolombangara and the other Central Solomon Islands were brought back to safer Japanese areas, they were concentrated on Bougainville. The staff of the IJA 17th Army evaluated the beach areas on Bougainville as potential landing sites for an amphibious invasion. Ironically, they rejected Cape Torokina at Empress Augusta Bay as most unlikely because of the low, swampy ground there. Only one company of 270 men from the 2nd Battalion/23rd IJA Infantry Regiment of the 6th Infantry Division with a single 75mm artillery piece was sent there to maintain an outpost. However, these Japanese troops were imbued with the emperor's wishes to defend every spot tenaciously, and this small force would mount a strong defence at Torokina.

General Masatane Kanda, commander of the IJA 6th Infantry Division, believed that the Allies would land east of Cape Torokina where he had about 2,500 troops in the area. Even after several days following the Marine invasion in Empress Augusta Bay, General Imamura on Rabaul still believed that the landing site at Torokina was short-lived. Imamura firmly believed that the Buka Island area was the main focus for Halsey's forces and, therefore, reinforced the northern tip of Bougainville rather than counter-attacking the Torokina beachhead with his substantial number of troops on the island. Later, despite the Allies' continued presence at Cape Torokina, he continued to build-up the defences at Buin on the southern tip of Bougainville.

Halsey's requirement for a Bougainville beachhead was enough territory that was not heavily defended in order to establish a strong perimeter, and to construct a fighter airstrip since continuous carrier-based air cover would not be available for the invasion site. Thereafter, additional airfields would be built further inland within an enlarged perimeter for medium-sized bombers. The Kieta area on Bougainville's east coast had the requisite flat plains for airfields as well as good harbours for Allied transports. However, this locale was near Japanese-occupied Choiseul, which meant that this large Solomon Island too would have to be secured in advance. Disadvantages to other beaches on Bougainville's east coast were their proximity to strong Japanese garrisons concentrated in the island's southern tip at Buin as well as poor soil composition for airfield construction. An alternative site for Halsey's planning staff was at Cape Torokina in Empress Augusta Bay on Bougainville's west coast. It was closer to Rabaul than Kieta and its approach was unimpeded by adjacent enemy-held islands or strong garrisons. A 5-mile strip of beach there was deemed suitable for a landing with nearby soil conditions favourable for building airfields. Marines had secretly landed on Bougainville's west coast from the US Navy submarine *Guardfish*, and found that soil samples similar to that at Cape Torokina were suitable for the construction of airfields. As to other potential landing beaches on Bougainville's west coast, these were backed by extensive swamps, which would preclude airfield construction and troop manoeuvring to develop a stout perimeter. Finally, given the primitive jungle trails and the harsh mountainous terrain of the Emperor and Crown Prince Mountain Ranges, the Cape Torokina area was, in essence, almost isolated from the strong Japanese garrisons in northern and southern Bougainville. Halsey's staff calculated that it would take the Japanese three to four months to bring enough heavy artillery over the mountains to launch massive counter-attacks against a strong American perimeter fortified ashore at Empress Augusta Bay.

On the downside, Empress Augusta Bay's inshore waters were poorly charted and treacherous with the 5-mile strip of beach largely unprotected from monsoons. Also, the terrain's low, swampy coastline and the bay's anchorage, which was unsuitable for large vessels, were deficiencies of this landing area. Finally, the Torokina area was no further than 65 miles from any of the Japanese air-bases on Bougainville, and only 215 miles from Rabaul's airdromes to the north-west.

On 22 September 1943, Halsey cancelled all his earlier invasion plans and assigned the units to constitute Bougainville's invasion force. The 14,000 men of the newly formed 3rd Marine Division, reinforced by the 2nd and 3rd Marine Raider Battalions and the 3rd Marine Defence Battalion, would lead the assault at Empress Augusta Bay. In sharp contrast to the assault on New Georgia in the Central Solomons, Halsey would send his troops ashore at the weakly held Cape Torokina area, despite having beach and terrain conditions that the admiral pronounced as 'worse than anything ever encountered in the South Pacific'. Halsey informed MacArthur of his selected landing site at Cape Torokina on 1 October with an invasion via Empress Augusta Bay set for 1 November.

Rear Admiral Theodore S. Wilkinson would be Commander, Bougainville Amphibious Force Task Force 31. Along with Vandegrift and then Geiger, serving as Commanding General, IMAC, these experienced leaders would help overcome the deficiencies that faced the 3rd Marine Division (Reinforced) under Major General Allen Turnage, of which, according to the division's history, 'Virtually nothing was known of the hydrography, terrain conditions inland from selected beaches, and location of enemy defences in the immediate area,' largely due to the delayed selection of the Cape Torokina amphibious landing site. Although Vandegrift had obtained the requisite transport to land his 14,000 Marines, he was still anxious that there might be more than the 300 Japanese troops suspected to be in the immediate landing area. Follow-up convoys, after the initial landings at Torokina on 1 November 1943, were scheduled to deliver additional supplies as well as the 21st Marines, the 1st Marine Parachute Regiment and the US Army's 37th Infantry Division.

A preliminary naval bombardment of Cape Torokina and strafing of the landing beaches by navy dive-bombers from Munda on New Georgia began at 0600 hours on 1 November 1943, but drew no Japanese response. Then, assault waves of Marines from the 3rd Division, the 9th Marines on the left and the 3rd Marines on the right, crossed their narrow beaches of only 30–50 yards in depth to enter Bougainville's adjacent dense jungle. The 2nd Raider Battalion was in between battalions of the 3rd Marines close to Cape Torokina. Elements of the 3rd Raider Battalion seized Puruata Island, which was situated in Empress Augusta Bay to the north-west of Cape Torokina and was adjacent to Torokina Island laying in the bay to its east. The landing beaches in length comprised roughly 8,000 yards and extended from Cape Torokina to just west of the Koromokina Lagoon, which was fed by a similarly named river. Although not encountering strong Japanese forces, heavy surf as well as a high beach mitigated proper anchoring of many of the 9th Marines' landing

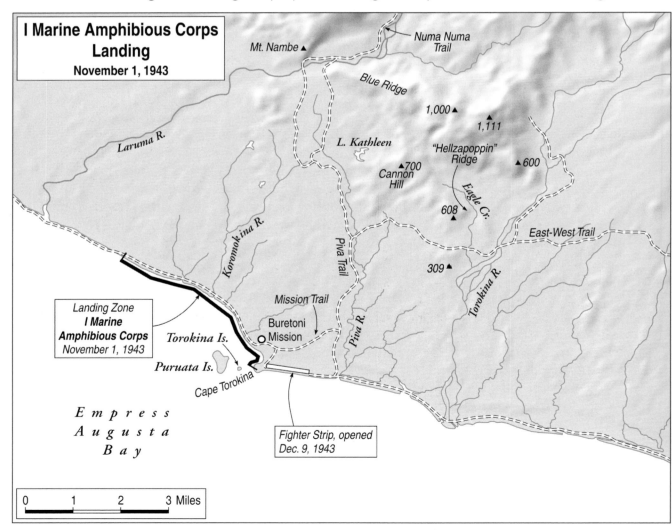

I Marine Amphibious Corps Landing
November 1, 1943

Mt. Nambe ▲

Numa Numa Trail

Blue Ridge

1,000 ▲
1,111 ▲

L. Kathleen

"Hellzapoppin" Ridge
▲ 600

Laruma R.

▲ 700
Cannon Hill

Eagle Cr.

608 ▲

East-West Trail

309 ▲

Koromokina R.

Piva Trail

Torokina R.

Mission Trail

Landing Zone
I Marine Amphibious Corps
November 1, 1943

Buretoni Mission

Torokina Is.

Piva R.

Puruata Is.

Cape Torokina

Empress Augusta Bay

Fighter Strip, opened Dec. 9, 1943

0   1   2   3 Miles

craft on the western or left flank beaches, forcing many to wade ashore in deep water to the far left of the assault beaches. With over eighty Landing Craft Vehicles, Personnel (LCVPs) and Landing Craft Mechanized (LCMs) disabled, Vandegrift, the IMAC commander, halted further landings along the 9th Marines beaches.

However, to the far right of the assault beaches, the 1st Battalion/3rd Marines ran into over twenty-five Japanese entrenched positions on Cape Torokina, which were only minimally damaged by the preceding naval bombardment. In addition, there was a 75mm artillery piece, protected by machine-gun pillboxes and infantry rifle pits, on the northern face of the cape enfilading the amphibious assault of the 1st Battalion/3rd Marines and the 2nd Raider Battalion at a range of only 500 yards. This entrenched Japanese 75mm gun hit fourteen landing craft, of which four sank, and disrupted the proper landing sites of the battalions' companies and headquarters. The 2nd and 3rd Battalions/3rd Marines made easier landing on their beaches as there were no Japanese fortifications to their front and the few enemy troops there fled into the jungle after only token resistance.

Sergeant Robert A. Owens and his squad from A Company, 1st Battalion/3rd Marines attacked the Japanese 75mm artillery piece situated in a palm log bunker

Map 4. The amphibious assault by I Marine Amphibious Corps (IMAC) in Empress Augusta Bay occurred on 1 November 1943 against entrenched Japanese defensive positions on the Marines' right flank at Cape Torokina as well as on Puruata Island. After a shallow 4,000-yard beachhead was secured on D-Day, combat along a jungle perimeter extended from well to the south of the Laruma River to oppose an enemy movement from the north to positions on the Mission Trail should the Japanese approach from the south. US Navy 'Seabees' began building rudimentary roads and a coastal fighter strip at Cape Torokina on 10 November, which was finished on 9 December. Within days of securing the beachhead, a company of Marine raiders established a road-block along the Piva Trail. Marine and Army reinforcements joined the perimeter defence from 6–9 November. A limited Japanese counter-attack to the south of the Laruma River was defeated by the Marines on 8 November at the Battle of the Koromokina River. A stronger Japanese counter-attack from Buin was hurled at the Piva Trail road-block on the right of the perimeter on 7–8 November. The Marines continued to expand the perimeter to the crossroads of the Piva, Numa Numa and east–west trails on 13 November, in order to enable the Americans to begin building two more airfields within it. On 19–20 November, the Marines moved to seize some of the high ground heading north-eastwards from the Torokina beaches. However, after some Marine units crossed the Piva River and headed east for roughly 1,000 yards, they encountered an impenetrable swamp. On 24 November, the 3rd Marines advanced in the direction of Eagle Creek and the Torokina River to the east of the Piva River branches against fierce and determined Japanese opposition in defensive fortifications. Another mile beyond their intended objective, the Marines again became bogged down in swampland. Among other topographic features that required seizure by the Marines, in order to protect the future inland American bomber and fighter airfields' construction sites from shelling, was Hill 608 north of the East–West Trail astride Eagle Creek. On 7 December, elements from the Marines 1st Parachute Regiment slowly attempted to occupy a spur adjoining Hill 608, only to be beaten back by the enemy. After eleven days of savage fighting for what would become known as 'Hellzapoppin Ridge', elements of the 21st Marines finally took this slope. On 21 December, other elements of the 21st Marines drove the enemy off of Hill 600, which was near the Torokina River. These actions to secure the limited heights above Bougainville's jungle floor ended the combat mission for the Marines on the island, which, with the support of elements of the Army's 37th Infantry Division, had penetrated over 22,000 yards from the narrow beaches. (*Philip Schwartzberg, Meridian Mapping*)

with sand-filled aviation fuel drums reinforcing the structure. Owens had observed the devastating effect that the Japanese gun was having on the beach and approaching landing craft. While sending four men to put suppressive fire on adjacent bunkers to the gun's position, Owens ran up-hill to storm the artillery bunker single-handedly, despite being hit by Japanese Arisaka 6.6mm-calibre rifle fire from enemy snipers. Other members of his squad at the base of the hill above the landing area were also felled by sniper fire. After reaching the bunker's gun port, Owens crawled through the aperture firing his Thompson .45 calibre submachine-gun, killing several of the artillery crew. Escaping members of the Japanese artillery piece, exiting through the rear of the bunker, were killed by other Marines. When Owens too emerged through the rear exit of the bunker, he collapsed and died from wounds received while charging the bunker. The bunker had an abundance of high explosive (HE) ammunition that would have been fired at the beach and landing craft had Owens not killed most of the crew. Owens received the Congressional Medal of Honor, posthumously, for his bravery and sacrifice. The other pillboxes were all destroyed by the afternoon by similar assaults with suppressive fire at the opening of the fortifications that enabled other Marines to either force hand-grenades down the ventilation shafts or assault the rear of the structures.

In the communication trenches between the pillboxes, Marines resorted to hand-to-hand combat with the Japanese 23rd Infantry Regiment defenders. Over half of the 270 Japanese infantrymen in the 2nd Company from this regiment eventually fled into the jungle, while the Marines suffered 180 killed and wounded. Puruata and Torokina Islands were taken by the 3rd Raider Battalion with minimal casualties, but requiring a few additional days to root out snipers.

The battle for the narrow beachhead had ended, but combat along the jungle perimeter was now to begin with G Company of the 9th Marines situated well to the south of the Laruma River to oppose an enemy movement from the north, while M Company of the 3rd Raider Battalion, that was attached to the 2nd Raider Battalion for the main landing, took up positions on the Mission Trail should the Japanese approach from the south. Japanese air attacks from Rabaul commenced immediately after the landings started, which briefly suspended operations, as American fighters from Vella Lavella and Munda engaged the Japanese 'Val' dive-bombers and 'Zero' fighter escort numbering about 120 planes that day. By the end of 1 November, the 75mm and 105mm Howitzers of the 12th Marines were hauled through Bougainville's muck into the perimeter, while the 90mm AA guns of the 3rd Marine Defence Battalion dug-in to give the Marines ashore some added firepower to the more than 14,000 Marines that had landed. During the first several days after the amphibious assault, US Navy 'Seabees' began constructing some rudimentary roadways and started work on a fighter strip at Cape Torokina.

The US Navy's cruiser and destroyer divisions would also be heavily engaged by IJN surface vessels on 1–2 November. A second Japanese task force under Admiral Kurita; including heavy cruisers, light cruisers and destroyers, was attacked by a daring carrier plane air-strike launched from the *Saratoga* and *Princeton* on Rabaul's Simpson Harbor on 5 November, where the enemy ships were refuelling. Of the seven Japanese heavy cruisers in the harbour, four were severely damaged during the just over 20-minute raid, thereby preventing a potential interdiction of Marine resupply at Cape Torokina that would have been reminiscent of the first few days at Guadalcanal.

After Marine patrolling could find no significant Japanese formations in the immediate 2-mile vicinity of the temporary perimeter as the first week after the landings came to an end, the positions of the 3rd and 9th Marines were reversed by General Turnage. The raiders from Puruata and Torokina Islands were held in reserve except for one company placed at a road-block along the Piva Trail. Marine reinforcements, in the form of elements of the 21st Marines, arrived in the perimeter on 6 November, while the 148th Infantry Regiment of the army's 37th Division landed on 9 November. Within two additional weeks, the 37th Division's artillery along with its 129th and 145th Regiments would also land.

The Japanese had been confused about the site of Bougainville's invasion and also underestimated the strength of the lodgement, as they had previously done at Guadalcanal. The IJA 17th Army Headquarters, led by Lieutenant General Hyakutake, had given up the defensive initiative at Torokina, believing that the major American landing would still occur at Buka in the north or Buin on the island's southern tip. Hyakutake received elements of the 17th IJA Division's 53rd and 54th Infantry Regiments from Rabaul, which landed on Bougainville on 7 November, to engage the left of the Marine perimeter as to force commitment of Marine reserves, while the stronger attack from Buin would be hurled at the Piva Trail road-block on the right of the perimeter. The Japanese landings were scattered by the heavy surf to the north of the perimeter and, rather than wait to consolidate the forces, as with the attacks on the Marine perimeter on Guadalcanal, the Japanese chose to immediately attack K Company of the 3rd Battalion/9th Marines near the Laruma River. A Marine machine-gun emplacement along a jungle track initially repelled an attack by roughly 100 Japanese infantrymen, for which PFC Challis Still, who gallantly manned the machine-gun, would win a Silver Star. After the failed Japanese attack, the remainder of the Marine K Company was ordered to counter-attack through deep swamp by its battalion commander, which compelled the enemy to go onto the defensive just west of the Koromokina River.

The attacking K Company Marines had exhausted themselves trying to evict the Japanese from their impromptu defensive positions and were relieved by company-sized elements of the 1st Battalion/3rd Marines, supported by tanks and 37mm artillery pieces, which destroyed some of the enemy emplacements. Two Marines from B Company, the commander, Captain Gordon Warner, and Sergeant Herbert J. Thomas, won the Navy Cross and a posthumous Medal of Honor respectively for their heroism in wiping out Japanese entrenchments. The next day, 8 November, commenced with an attack by the 1st Battalion/21st Marines, which had recently landed, supported by 12th Marines' artillery barrage and a combined mortar and tank attack by the 1st Battalion/3rd Marines. Only limited Japanese opposition was found and American air-strikes near the Laruma River's mouth added to about 300 enemy killed at this battle of the Koromokina, while the Marines suffered over forty-five killed and wounded.

A Japanese thrust had also been anticipated to come from the south in the vicinity of the Piva Trail, where elements of the 2nd Raider Battalion blocked the track. Battalion-sized formations of the IJA 23rd Infantry Regiment of the 6th Division from Buin attacked on 7–8 November. Led by Major General Shun Iwasa, a Japanese frontal attack was launched but halted by the Marine raiders, supported by the mortar men of the 9th Marines. General Turnage, still in need of expanding his perimeter to the south, sent in the 3rd Raider Battalion along both the Piva and Numa Numa trails on the morning of 9 November. A stalemate developed between both sides for several hours until after a failed Japanese envelopment, the enemy retreated through Piva Village, which was eventually taken that day by the 1st and 2nd Battalions/ 9th Marines. In addition, the Marines were now at the junction of the Piva, Numa Numa and east–west trails. Control of these crossroads would enable the Marines to begin building their airfields while keeping the Japanese outside the perimeter. This combat cost the Marines just over fifty killed and wounded, while over 500 dead Japanese were found. As on Guadalcanal, Japanese assaults on the Marine perimeter on Bougainville had been uncoordinated and without massed forces, probably a result of underestimating the strength of the Marines ashore.

On 13 November, the 2nd Battalion/21st Marines moved beyond the crossroads to set up an outpost, under the command of Lieutenant Colonel Eustace Smoak. Proper reconnaissance was not performed by the advancing Marines, who ran into a well-armed reinforced company-sized enemy detachment in a coconut grove with strong defensive fortifications. Due to the terrain, the Marine battalion's companies lost contact with one another as well as with the battalion headquarters. Despite Marine dive-bomber and artillery bombardment of the coconut grove the next morning, the Japanese were able to maintain their positions there. Supported by M3 light tanks of the 3rd Tank Battalion, two Marine companies advanced in a frontal assault. However, accurate Japanese anti-tank (AT) gunfire ambushed the Marines and disrupted the attack. By the end of the day, the Japanese retreated eastward on the East–West Trail. Over forty Japanese bodies were found among some shattered fortifications, but there were also about sixty Marines killed and wounded.

Reinforcements in the form of the 3rd Battalion/21st Marines, along with the 148th and 129th Infantry Regiments of the US Army's 37th Division, enabled expansion of the perimeter by about 1,000 to 1,500 yards along the centre and left while the swamp at the right side was maintained by the 9th Marines. Unfortunately, Japanese air attacks had caused significant casualties among reinforcements offshore as well and within the perimeter on 17 November. With Nimitz's Central Pacific offensive in the Gilbert Islands and MacArthur's SWPA troops advancing westward into Netherlands New Guinea, the South Pacific Force's jungle fighting along the Bougainville defensive perimeter was about to become overshadowed by these other campaigns.

Although the crossroads of Bougainville's main trails were in Marine possession, the Japanese still maintained road-blocks on them further inland. Marine General Geiger, now in command of IMAC, wanted to expand the perimeter further by clearing the road-blocks on the Numa Numa Trail, paralleling the Piva River's West Branch, and the East–West Trail where it comes into proximity with the former trail and a tributary of the Piva River's East Branch. Also, Geiger wanted to seize some of the high ground heading north-eastwards from the Torokina beaches. These attacks on the trails' road-blocks were successfully put in by the 2nd and 3rd Battalions/ 3rd Marines on 19–20 November. When Lieutenant Steve Cibik's platoon from F Company of the 2nd Battalion/3rd Marines was ordered to seize a 400–500 foot ridge just north of the East–West Trail overlooking the Piva River branches on 21 November, a sharp engagement occurred with the Japanese trying to retake the ridge. After three days of Japanese suicide charges, an additional 200 Marine reinforcements and countless direct fire-support artillery missions landing within 50 yards of Cibik's positions, the ridge remained in the 3rd Marines' hands enabling the perimeter to advance north-eastwards.

Also, on 21 November, other Marine units crossed the Piva River and headed east for roughly 1,000 yards until they encountered an impenetrable swamp. The army's 37th Division's 129th Regiment, moving on the far left of the perimeter, was able to advance 1,000 yards to the north-west without any opposition. On 24 November, an extensive preliminary Marine and army artillery and mortar barrage was unleashed for a 3rd Marines' advance in the direction of Eagle Creek and the Torokina River to the east of the Piva River branches against fierce and determined Japanese opposition in defensive fortifications. However, the Marines advanced almost a mile beyond their intended objective, again becoming situated in swampland. During this combat, the Marines incurred over 100 casualties, while the Japanese left tenfold more dead on the shell-pocked battlefield.

Other topographic features that required seizure by the Marines, in order to protect the future inland American bomber and fighter airfields' construction sites from shelling, were Hill 608, just to the north of the East–West Trail, and Hill 600, east of Eagle Creek moving towards the Torokina River. On 7 December, elements from the Marines' 1st Parachute Regiment slowly attempted to occupy a spur adjoining Hill 608, only to be beaten back by a reinforced company from the Japanese 23rd Infantry Regiment using determined machine-gun, rifle and mortar fire from their entrenchments. After eleven days of savage fighting for what would become known as 'Hellzapoppin Ridge', elements of the 21st Marines finally took this slope but required air-strikes from the newly activated Torokina coastal fighter airstrip, which the 'Seabees' began constructing on 10 November and finished on 9 December, as well as 12th Marines' 155mm Howitzer fire from a battery near the Torokina River to evict the Japanese, who left more than fifty dead in their reverse slope positions. Fortunately, the Marines suffered only thirty-five killed and wounded, since the ferocity of the combat was severe. On 21 December, other elements of the 21st Marines drove the enemy off of Hill 600, which was also near the Torokina River, but upon their withdrawal for the night, the Japanese returned necessitating three more days of attacks before the Japanese retired from the hill.

These actions to secure the limited heights above Bougainville's jungle floor ended the combat mission for the Marines on Bougainville, which, with the support of the Army's 37th Infantry Division, had penetrated this northern Solomon Island's jungle over 22,000 yards from the narrow beaches stormed over seven weeks earlier. General Geiger's IMAC command was replaced by Major General Oscar W. Griswold, now commanding the US Army's XIVth Corps. The Americal Division, under the command of Major General John R. Hodge, replaced most of the 3rd Marine Division, the latter unit departing Bougainville on 25 December, after having suffered over 400 killed and 1,400 men wounded. The 9th and 21st Marines left the island on 28 December 1943 and 9 January 1944 respectively. Hyakutake's forces had 2,500 dead accounted for on the battlefield with only twenty-five of the enemy being captured as a testament to the suicidal tenacity of the Japanese *bushido* code. In order to create combat veteran nuclei for the new Marine divisions in the expanding six-division Marine Corps, all of the raider and Marine Paratroop units were disbanded in early 1944.

The mission to seize Torokina achieved fruition when, on 26 November, construction began on a bomber airfield, *Piva Uncle*, and a second fighter strip, *Piva Yoke*, both of which enabled aircraft flying from the Central Solomon Islands airfields to stage their missions to neutralize Rabaul. Halsey, in saluting his Marines, stated to Geiger, 'You have literally succeeded in setting up and opening for business a shop in the Japs' front yard.'

Marine Lieutenant General Alexander A. Vandegrift (*second from right*) confers with Navy Commander E.J. Moran (*far left*), Army XIVth Corps Commander Major General O.W. Griswold (*second from left*) and Marine Major General Ralph Mitchell, head of the Solomons air command. Vandegrift, who won the Congressional Medal of Honor for his leadership of the 1st Marine Division (Reinforced) on Guadalcanal, would briefly be in command of the I Marine Amphibious Corps (IMAC), which would assault Bougainville at Cape Torokina in Empress Augusta Bay on 1 November 1943, until Marine Major General Roy Geiger, another Guadalcanal veteran, arrived from Washington. Griswold would take over command of troops on Bougainville in early 1944 and lead the Torokina perimeter defence by the Americal and 37th Infantry Divisions against the Japanese counter-attack in March 1944. (*USAMHI*)

Commodore Lawrence F. Reifsnider, USN (*left*) and Marine 3rd Division Commanding Officer, Major General Allen Turnage (*right*) aboard a transport on 31 October 1943, the day before the invasion of Bougainville at Cape Torokina in Empress Augusta Bay. Reifsnider was in charge of the Transport Group, which would get the 3rd Division Marines to Empress Augusta Bay in combat-loaded transports and cargo ships. The overall command of the III Amphibious Force, Task Force 31, Main Body, Northern Force was under Rear Admiral Thomas S. Wilkinson (*not shown*). Wilkinson had taken over command of amphibious landings from Rear Admiral R. Kelly Turner. Prior to that, Wilkinson had worked for Halsey as Deputy Commander, South Pacific. Both naval commanders knew about the supply problems on Guadalcanal and in the Central Solomons, so the aim for the Bougainville invasion would be to get the men and supplies out of the transports and cargo ships with the vessels leaving those waters before the inevitable Japanese air and naval force counter-attack. (*USMC*)

Vice Admiral William F. Halsey (*left*), wearing tropical sun helmet, decorates Marine Generals Roy Geiger (*centre*) and Allen H. Turnage (*right*) after the successful landings and initial defence of the Bougainville Perimeter at Cape Torokina. Geiger, a Marine aviator who commanded Marine aviation on Guadalcanal, had taken over I Marine Amphibious Corps (IMAC) after succeeding Vandegrift, the latter having been promoted for a Marine Corps command position in Washington. Geiger wanted to expand Turnage's 3rd Marine Division outposts on the trails emanating from the Torokina beachhead as well as have the building of airstrips as a top priority. In order to construct the airfields in the proposed sites, he would have to clear out the Japanese and build the roads for supply of the front lines. Turnage commanded the 14,000 troops of the reinforced 3rd Marine Division for the amphibious assault and preliminary occupation of the Torokina beachhead until Army units arrived. (*NARA*)

(**Opposite above**) Marines raiders clamber down the cargo nets over the side of a transport into a waiting Landing Craft, Personnel (LCP) for the assault on the beaches of Cape Torokina in Empress Augusta Bay on 1 November 1943. Note the Doberman pinscher (*to the right of cargo net*) also being loaded into the craft. The Bougainville invasion would mark the debut of dogs working alongside the Marine raiders during combat operations. (*NARA*)

(**Opposite below**) Five Landing Craft, Vehicle and Personnel (LCVPs) circle alongside a transport in Empress Augusta Bay to form up as an assault wave to land at Cape Torokina on Bougainville's southern coast on 1 November. Mount Bagana is in the centre of the background, flanked by nearby mountain ranges. Approximately 8,000 Marines were to be in the island's initial assault wave. (*USMC*)

(**Above**) Transports sit offshore of Cape Torokina in the background as Landing Craft, Vehicle and Personnel make ready for their run-in to the beachhead. Aboard a patrol torpedo (PT) boat in the foreground sits a gunner manning his twin 0.50-inch calibre machine-guns awaiting the inevitable Japanese fighter and bomber sweeps to disrupt the landings. (*USMC*)

(**Above**) A Landing Vehicle, Tracked (LVT), or 'Alligator', lies low in the water as it prepares to bring Marines from the 3rd Marine Division to the shoreline of Cape Torokina on D-Day, 1 November 1943. This shallow draft wooden vessel, which participated in the Guadalcanal campaign, was developed in the southern United States for use in the swampy Florida Everglades. (*NARA*)

(**Opposite above**) The LVT was an amphibian and, as such, could crawl onto the beach with its treads to bring the troops toward relative cover and serve to protect them with their array of machine-guns and, often, 20mm Polsen cannons. As shown, the beach at Cape Torokina was very narrow. (*NARA*)

(**Opposite below**) Marine from the 3rd Division in a Landing Craft, Vehicle and Personnel (LCVP) moves into position to land at Cape Torokina. As the assault boats moved closer to shore, they met fire from one of the offshore islets off the Cape Torokina beachhead, Puruata Island. A platoon of Japanese infantrymen, who were heavily armed with several heavy machine-guns, was stationed on this small island just to the west of the landing beaches. This small number of enemy soldiers had put up a murderous fire against the approaching landing craft to Torokina that simply headed straight to the beach, nonetheless. Only a squad of Japanese was on Torokina Island, midway between Puruata Island and Cape Torokina. (*NARA*)

(**Above**) Marines hunker down below the gunwales of their Landing Craft, Vehicle and Personnel (LCVP) as a naval shell explodes on the nearby shoreline in the upper left background. Although there were only 270 Japanese entrenched ashore at Cape Torokina, the enemy had a 75mm artillery piece, which was in range of the landing beaches. The Japanese fired roughly fifty high explosive shells at the approaching landing craft and did a good deal of damage. One landing craft alone, from one of the more proximate transports to the Japanese on Cape Torokina, the *President Adams*, received three direct hits from the entrenched enemy gun, which killed fifteen Marine and naval personnel, while wounding an additional fourteen. (*NARA*)

(**Opposite above**) With the bow ramp of a Landing Craft, Vehicle and Personnel (LCVP) down and implanted in the sand, Marines storm ashore at Cape Torokina on 1 November 1943. Those Marines farthest to the east met more intense enemy small arms, mortar and artillery fire. These Marines are approaching the shore upright as another LCVP in the assault wave approaches in the background. (*NARA*)

(**Opposite below**) Marines exit rapidly from their Landing Craft, Vehicle and Personnel (LCVP) onto an uncontested area of the Torokina beachhead. It is again evident how narrow the beach was at Torokina as some of the Marines are already preparing to enter dense jungle vegetation. Although the Japanese commanders of Bougainville had made some inferences, after finding American debris at beach locales prior the invasion, that Torokina was a potential landing site, only one company of the IJA 23rd Infantry Regiment of General Kanda's 6th Division would be entrenched in their defensive fortifications on D-Day. However, imbued with Tokyo's wishes to defend every spot tenaciously now, the opposition, although few in number, would mount a strong defence at Torokina. (*NARA*)

(**Opposite above**) Some Marines did not have a complete run-up to the shoreline on D-Day. Here a group is wading through the surf as seen from a beached landing craft in the foreground. The assault boat's 0.30-inch calibre Browning machine-gun is pointing skywards and is unmanned, suggesting that this was a more westerly undefended area of the Cape Torokina beachhead. (*NARA*)

(**Above**) Some areas of the Torokina landing beaches had rough surf on D-Day. Here Marines try to push a Landing Craft, Vehicle and Personnel (LCVP) that was stranded sideways on the beach back into the water (*foreground*) while another two seem to be stranded (*background*) with their bow ramps facing sideways and backwards facing the water. (*NARA*)

(**Opposite below**) A US Navy Scout Bomber Douglas (SBD) Dauntless dive-bomber flies cover over the beachhead on 1 November 1943. Mount Bagana and other heights loom high in the background at Cape Torokina. Transports and supporting destroyers are close to shore with nearby islets visible off the coast of Bougainville. Appearing as specks in the background, a flight of six navy planes flies parallel to the beachhead. At 0730 hours on D-Day, the predictable Japanese aerial response to the invasion with enemy bombers and fighters commenced. An American destroyer, the USS *Wadsworth*, which had been far to the east in line shelling the enemy emplacements on Cape Torokina, was hit with two fatalities and half a dozen sailors wounded. (*NARA*)

(**Above**) A group of Marines are hotly engaged at the jungle's edge at one of the more easterly landing sites, probably Blue Beach, where the Japanese had prepared defenses to protect the 270 enemy defenders at Cape Torokina on D-Day. Japanese gunfire had caused some mixing up of the 2nd Battalion of the 3rd Marines with the 2nd Raider Battalion. The assault boat crews, in response to the enemy fire, had hurried their run-in to the beach and landed at more proximate rather than intended points. (*Author's Collection*)

(**Opposite above left**) Marine raiders lie prone in some makeshift cover at the junction with the beach's edge and the dense vegetation of Bougainville's jungle on D-Day. The 3rd Battalion of the 2nd Raiders landed on Puruata Island with the mission to eliminate the platoon of Japanese soldiers with their heavy machine-guns, which had previously enfiladed the landing craft headed to the main landing beaches. The Japanese were dug-in and well-camouflaged in their entrenchments and it would take until 1200 hours on D-Day +1 to eliminate the enemy position with no prisoners being taken. (*NARA*)

(**Opposite above right**) A Marine in Bougainville's dense jungle foliage fires his Thompson 0.45-inch calibre submachine-gun at an enemy sniper position. Locating the enemy in their rifle pits and pillboxes was difficult, as these positions were well-camouflaged to blend in with the surrounding vegetation. (*USMC*)

Marines who have just exited from Torokina's narrow beachhead crouch in the nearby jungle trying to widen their position as a second assault wave prepares to hit the beach to complete the landing of D-Day's 8,000 3rd Division Marines. (*NARA*)

(**Above**) Two Marines warily scan through the jungle's vegetation to spot Japanese snipers. The Marine in the foreground holds his M1 Garand semi-automatic rifle while the one to the left holds his M1911 A1 0.45-inch calibre semi-automatic pistol at the ready. During the Second World War, Remington Rand made more than 900,000 M1911 A1 semi-automatic pistols. It was first issued in 1911 as the M1911 by Colt after being designed by John Browning. The pistol fired a .45 inch Automatic Colt Pistol (ACP) bullet from a 7-round magazine. It was termed a 'robust, reliable and efficient' gun with excellent stopping power. The maximal range of the pistol increased with model design from its inception and during the Second World War was just over 160 feet. (*NARA*)

(**Opposite above**) A Marine officer lies at the edge of the beach and jungle holding his M1 carbine as he scans the forward area for enemy positions, which were extremely difficult to spot almost until one was right on top of them due to the excellent enemy camouflage methods. The M1 Carbine semi-automatic 0.3 inch calibre rifle was originally borne out of the US Army's decision to develop an automatic weapon for troops not on the front line. The requirements were a more compact size than the M1 Garand, but more effective than a pistol or machine-pistol. Its production started in earnest from October 1941 onwards and the gun weighed 5.2lb unloaded and had a detachable 15- or 30-round magazine. The carbine could fire forty-five rounds per minute with an operational range just below 275 yards. Although the range and penetration force were less than for the M1 Garand, the M1 Carbine's lower weight along with a higher firing rate were favourable features for rear area and support troops. By 1945, over 6,000,000 had been manufactured. (*NARA*)

Sergeant Robert A. Owens of A Company 3rd Marines is shown before the invasion of Bougainville. Soon after landing on 1 November 1943, Owens led his squad to silence the 75mm artillery piece in a coconut log-fortified pillbox. Despite being wounded by sniper-fire, he managed to crawl through the gun port's aperture and fire his weapon killing most of the crew. The other Japanese in the pillbox, escaping through the rear exit, were soon killed by Owens' squad mates. However, Owens died from his wounds after exiting the pillbox. Owens received the Congressional Medal of Honor, posthumously, for his gallantry. If not silenced, the Japanese 75mm gun could have continued to wreak havoc on the Marines landing at Torokina since the pillbox had ample ammunition within the fortified position. (*Author's Collection*)

The rear exit to a Japanese pillbox at Torokina is shown. Not only could supplies be brought in without detection from the Front, but reinforcements could also come to the aid of such a position under attack by the Marines. (*NARA*)

Two Marines examine a Japanese pillbox housing a machine-gun from the rear after securing the beachhead on 1 November 1943. The structure has a roof fortified with coconut logs and is camouflaged with palm fronds on top. Aside from a direct hit by an artillery shell or aerial bomb, these enemy positions had to be reduced by direct assault or with TNT satchels thrown into them. (*NARA*)

Marines sit atop a small rise in the beach at Torokina (*far left*) as landing craft move about offshore (*background*). In the foreground, a dead Japanese soldier of the IJA 23rd Infantry Regiment of General Kanda's 6th Division lies sprawled with his helmet at his feet after fighting tenaciously to deny the Marines their beachhead. (*NARA*)

A Marine raider fires his M1 Garand semi-automatic rifle from behind a coconut tree at the enemy on Puruata Island. A platoon of Japanese with heavy machine-guns was situated on this island to the west of Cape Torokina and had raked assault craft making the run-in to the beachhead on D-Day. (*USMC*)

A quartet of Marines on Bougainville examines the dead body of a Japanese sniper not far from the tree that he had fallen from. In addition to trees, Japanese infantrymen lurked in well-camouflaged shallow rifle pits and 'spider holes' waiting for unsuspecting Marines to be in close proximity before opening fire. (*NARA*)

Soon after getting off the beach at Torokina on D-Day, the Marines began to expand their perimeter against any Japanese infantry counter-attack. Here, Marines set up a 0.50-inch calibre heavy machine-gun in front of a 37mm anti-tank gun, utility truck and Jeeps. (*NARA*)

Two Marines sit in a hastily improvised emplacement made with a tent half-sheet roof and a log embrasure housing their 0.30-inch calibre Browning water-cooled machine-gun with a muzzle flash suppressor. Such positions were established to guard trails where the enemy was expected to come down onto the beachhead from the hilly surrounding inland region. (*NARA*)

(**Opposite above**) Anticipating a rapid response from the Japanese air contingents from nearby airfields and Rabaul, members of the 3rd Marine Defence Battalion wait at the 40mm Bofors anti-aircraft gun emplacement shortly after the landings. (*NARA*)

(**Opposite below**) An M8 75mm pack Howitzer is manned by its crew from the 3rd Marine Defence Battalion as it prepares to fire on enemy positions. This versatile weapon was ideal for the jungles and mountainous terrain of the Pacific as it could be stripped down into its component parts in seconds for animal packs (thus the term 'pack Howitzer') or human transporting. The M8, with metal wheels and rubber tyres, was introduced in 1936. This artillery piece was relatively light, weighing 1,300lb, and fired high-explosive (HE) ammunition in support of infantry advances. This weapon was also quite adept at breaking up enemy formations on the counter-attack with its ordnance. (*USMC*)

(**Above**) Members of a 3rd Marine Defence Battalion crew are about to load a 90mm shell into their anti-aircraft gun near the Torokina beachhead. Japanese airmen respected the accuracy and destructive power of this weapon as the Marines set them up quickly upon landing to defend against the anticipated enemy aerial sorties. (*NARA*)

Marines form a human chain to move boxes of ammunition from a Landing Craft, Vehicle and Personnel (LCVP) at the shoreline onto the back of a truck's flatbed to move the supplies to the expanding Marine perimeter inland from the beach. (*NARA*)

(**Opposite above**) As with previous operations in the Southern and Central Solomon Islands, the movements of supplies from the beachhead inland to avoid exposure to enemy air attacks continued at Bougainville. Here Marine work details labour, after securing the Torokina landing beaches, to unload supplies and ammunitions across the depressed bow ramps of Navy Landing Craft, Vehicle and Personnel (LCVPs). (*NARA*)

(**Opposite below**) A 0.75-ton utility truck, which has just been loaded with munitions, begins to move across the beachhead through some deep sand. It appears that the front tyres may have chains on them to facilitate exiting from the beach to inland storage areas and the front lines. (*NARA*)

Marines assist in offloading a M3 half-track serving as a 75mm gun mounted carriage (GMC) from a Landing Craft, Vehicle and Personnel (LCVP) in a subsequent landing wave at Torokina. This was the primary American heavy tank destroyer in combat during 1942–1943, and it suffered from a very limited traverse and its cross-country speed was deemed inadequate. However, neither of these detriments would be applicable to fighting on the South Pacific Islands. (NARA)

Marines sit aboard their M3 half-track serving as a 75mm gun-mounted carriage (GMC) with their M1 Carbines at the ready. The front tyres have chains to facilitate this armoured vehicle leaving the beach at Cape Torokina. The 75mm gun was of First World War vintage, utilizing the French M1897 design as this M3 GMC was a hasty improvement over its vastly inferior predecessor, the M6 37mm GMC. (NARA)

Four Marines carry a litter bearing one of their wounded comrades from the jungle to the beach for evacuation by a landing craft to an offshore transport for more intricate medical care. (*NARA*)

A wounded Marine with his head bandaged lies outside a forward aid station or field hospital on Bougainville, where a surgeon is conducting the amputation of a limb. The mission of these forward medical aid stations was to stop haemorrhaging, remove devitalized tissue, apply sulphonamide antibiotic powder and dress the wound as well as administer narcotic analgesia. Subsequent wound care would commence after evacuation to rear echelon areas or aboard ship. Rifles stand against palm trees in the event of enemy infiltration, which was an incessant tactic of the Japanese on the South Pacific Islands. (*NARA*)

A Japanese aerial bomb has just hit a Marine supply dump inland from the beach and sends a smoke plume billowing skyward as attempts are made to douse the fires. The 3rd Division Marines would learn in their combat debut that there was no safe rear echelon area at the Cape Torokina beachhead on Bougainville. (NARA)

After the beach landings are secured, Marines move inland along one of the jungle trails to search for the enemy up in the mountains. Of the 270 Japanese defending Cape Torokina on D-Day, 192 enemy bodies were found. A detachment of the 3rd Marine Raider Battalion was to establish a road-block on the Piva Trail to the north-east of the Torokina beachhead. (NARA)

A patrol of Marine raiders moves out into the jungle with a new weapon, the aggressive Doberman pinscher. These dogs succeeded in their assigned task of sniffing out enemy snipers and concealed dugouts. For the initial few days after the landings, action was confined to patrols to ferret out lurking Japanese. (*NARA*)

A contingent of Marine raiders poses in front of a Japanese dug-out that was captured in the vicinity of the Cape Torokina beachhead. (*NARA*)

(**Above**) A Landing Vehicle, Tracked (LVT), or 'Alligator', moves inland with a 0.30-inch and 0.50-inch calibre machine-gun at the ready. The beachhead had to be expanded as the terrain around Torokina was comprised of swamp and dense jungle. Forward movement was measured in yards per hour even in the absence of enemy resistance. (*NARA*)

(**Opposite above**) A Marine M3 Stuart light tank courses through some dense jungle vegetation. Despite the terrain's obstacle, these tanks had succeeded in moving through jungle and coconut groves on both Guadalcanal and New Georgia earlier in the campaign. However, Marines on foot were needed to minimize Japanese infantry attacks on the armour. (*NARA*)

(**Opposite below**) A Marine M3 Stuart light tank in the lead with a squad of Marines behind it is ambushed by the Japanese at the junction of the Piva and Mission Trails towards the end of the first week of November 1943. A wounded Marine lies on the jungle floor in the left foreground. (*NARA*)

Marines fire their 0.30-inch calibre Browning light machine-gun from a water-filled foxhole along one of the trails emanating from the Torokina beachhead. Both Marines are wearing their full kit packs, suggesting that this position was hurriedly established while trekking along the jungle trail. (*NARA*)

(**Opposite above**) Marine raiders trudge through a typical jungle swamp as they patrol eastwards from the Cape Torokina perimeter to the Piva River, towards the end of the first week of November. Near the junction of the Piva and Mission trails, where Marine raiders had established a block on the trail, reinforcing elements of the IJA 23rd Infantry Regiment, which had crossed over to the west of the Piva River, were counter-attacked by elements of the 3rd Marine Raider Battalion and the 9th Marines on 9 November. Thereafter, this Japanese unit fought a series of delaying actions along the Numa Numa Trail before retiring to the safety of high ground to the east along the East–West Trail. (*NARA*)

(**Opposite below**) A Marine patrol shoots at Japanese snipers while some of the others prepare to fire a light artillery piece at the enemy. In their retreat along the Piva Trail during the second week of November, elements of the Japanese 23rd Infantry Regiment had abandoned much of their equipment, including small calibre artillery pieces, machine-guns, mortars and rifles. (*USMC*)

Marines set up their 0.50-inch calibre heavy machine-gun along a jungle trail inland from the Torokina beachhead. Several boxes of ammunition are in the foreground. Other Marines are cutting down some of the vegetation to develop foxholes and good fields of fire as they await a Japanese counter-attack. (NARA)

Marines manning a variety of weapons are involved in repelling a Japanese jungle assault. In the foreground, a Marine holds his 0.45-inch calibre Thompson submachine-gun, which was designed during the First World War, with the intent of providing infantry squads with a heavy, mobile fire-support weapon to breach enemy trenches – a 'trench cleaner' – firing the .45-inch ACP round. It was heavy, weighing almost 11lb empty, and could use box or drum magazines of 20, 30, 50 or 100 rounds. The Thompson had a maximal operation range of about 220 yards. The two centre Marines are ready to fire their 0.30-inch calibre Browning M1917 water-cooled, belt-fed heavy machine-gun. As its designation suggests, this machine-gun was produced in time for service with the American Expeditionary Force (AEF) in France during the First World War. However, its service life extended for more than half a century, having earned respect as an excellent defensive weapon in the jungles of Guadalcanal and New Georgia with a cyclic firing rate of up to 600 rounds per minute. With a weight of almost 33lb, this machine-gun was usually situated in a fixed position and required the bulk of its crew to move it for tactical reasons. The Marine in the background holds his M1 carbine at the ready to fire. (*NARA*)

A Marine sits on watch alongside his 0.30-inch calibre Browning light machine-gun at an outpost along a trail beyond the Torokina beachhead as the Marines sought to expand their perimeter as well as seek out a site for a proposed bomber airfield to the north to be constructed after a fighter strip was operational along the shoreline. (*NARA*)

A Marine patrol moves through almost knee-deep mud as the 3rd Division commanders attempt to reconnoitre enemy forces as part of a plan to expand the perimeter. Terrain such as this made lateral movement within the small perimeter after the Torokina landings ineffective. (*NARA*)

Elements of the 3rd Battalion/ 9th Marines make their way back to the Torokina perimeter after the action at the Piva Trail block against units from the Japanese 23rd Infantry Regiment in early to mid-November 1943. The Japanese had faced overwhelming American artillery firepower supporting the Marines, which compelled them to withdraw well to the east of the Piva River. (NARA)

The 1st Battalion/3rd Marines exit the jungle to return to the Torokina beachhead. The Japanese had not mounted a serious counter-attack against the main Marine perimeter at Torokina, with the exception of the Piva Road battles, as their commanders believed the main American assault on Bougainville would come elsewhere. (NARA)

(**Above**) Bougainville's Mt Bagana, an active volcano, stands high in the background as viewed from 'Hellzapoppin Ridge', the latter terrain feature being located to the north-east of the Marine perimeter at Torokina and was situated between the Piva and Torokina Rivers just to the north of the East–West Trail. Hellzapoppin Ridge was a 300-yard-long spur with steep slopes that extended eastward from a target map reference called 'Hill 608'. Hellzapoppin Ridge was not shown on any of the I Marine Amphibious Corps (IMAC) headquarters maps. Marines occupying other nearby hills had not noted any Japanese troops on the spur, although several empty but well dug-in emplacements were observed on 7 December. The following day, elements of the Marine 3rd Parachute Battalion moved onto the spur only to encounter a reinforced company of 200 enemy soldiers from the Japanese 23rd Infantry Regiment that reclaimed their fortified entrenchments the previous night and were now tenaciously holding onto the terrain feature. It would take almost a dozen days of intense combat before the Japanese withdrew, after which the Marine paratroopers assigned the spur the moniker Hellzapoppin Ridge. (*NARA*)

(**Opposite page**) Some rather haggard and harried-looking Marines haul cases of hand-grenades up the slopes of Hill 1000 in December 1943. I Marine Amphibious Corps (IMAC) commander, General Geiger, wanted this high ground, as well as some other less prominent hills, to deny the Japanese access from which they periodically shelled the beachhead and the newly built fighter airstrip on Cape Torokina's shoreline. (*NARA*)

(**Opposite above**) Crewmen of a Marine Defence Battalion service their M3 light Stuart tanks after some recent combat. This light armour, although antiquated by European standards, proved vital when combined with infantry to reduce Japanese entrenchments in the jungle. (*NARA*)

(**Opposite below**) Marines hammer logs together while constructing a bridge that will traverse one of the many waterways, such as the Laruma, Koromokina, Piva and Torokina Rivers that empty into Empress Augusta Bay as they descend from nearby mountain ranges. (*NARA*)

(**Above**) Marines rest atop a log-reinforced bridge across an inland gully that could probably support small vehicles, such as Jeeps. To bridge other waterways, disabled amphibious assault craft, LVTs, were sometimes used as pontoons. (*NARA*)

(**Opposite above**) As two Marines stand guard, others string telephone wire from one tree to another that have been denuded of their palm fronds. Since the 1 November landings, Navy 'Seabees' had been busy building roads through the jungle from the beachhead as attested to by the presence of a nearby Jeep. (*NARA*)

(**Above**) Bougainville's ubiquitous mud, as on all of the other Solomon Islands invaded by the Allies, forces Marines to manhandle a cart that carries ammunition from a storage area to the front lines. Due to the depth of the morass, two half-track vehicles sit stationary in the right background. (*USMC*)

(**Opposite below**) Marines are shown knee-deep in mud as they try to utilize a bulldozer to bring artillery rounds in a tracked cart to the front lines. Some of the worst terrain, including tidal swamps, was often near the coastal zones. American Marines and soldiers fighting in the Solomon Islands often described the mud as having an unpleasant dank smell – perhaps from the volcanic soil common to those islands. The female anopheles mosquito thrives in such stagnant pools and Bougainville was no exception to being a reservoir for the malarial parasite transmitted by this biting insect. (*NARA*)

So when we reach the "Isle of Japan"
With our caps at a Jaunty tilt
We'll enter the city of Tokyo
On the roads the SEABEES Built.

Third Marine
2ⁿᵈ Raider R

The Fighter Strip at Cape Torokina's shoreline as seen in late 1944 from an aircraft flying over it. Eight 'Seabee' battalions and one New Zealand engineer brigade began work on a fighter strip at the edge of Cape Torokina on a relatively dry area in Empress Augusta Bay on 10 November 1943. Remarkably, the fighter strip was ready for operation on 10 December, when Marine F4U Corsairs flew into their new base. (*NARA*)

(**Opposite above**) A Marine (*right*) and a Navy 36th Construction Battalion worker or 'Seabee' (*left*) congratulate each other on the completion of a major road bearing a long line of Jeeps and other military vehicles with a drainage ditch to the side. Working in combat areas was not new for the 'Seabees'. The 'Seabees' were recruited by the navy from the ranks of the American construction industry. In addition to some much-needed roads on Bougainville, the 'Seabees' located a site suitable for a bomber strip in the dense jungle north of the beachhead in the waning days of November 1943. By 19 December, after clearing the vegetation and tree stumps, levelling and grading the earth, and adding sections of Marston matting and crushed coral, the first plane flew off the 8,000-foot runway of *Piva Uncle* for a bombing sortie. Secretary of the Navy, James Forrestal commented in 1945, 'The Seabees have carried the war in the Pacific on their backs'. (*USMC*)

(**Opposite below**) A Marine F4U Corsair, with its characteristic inverted gull-like wing configuration, takes off for a mission from the Fighter Strip at Cape Torokina. The first time the Torokina fighter airstrip was used against Rabaul was on 17 December 1943, when almost eighty fighters from New Georgia staged through it. A bomber airstrip, *Piva Uncle*, was started on 29 November and was operational by 19 December. An additional fighter strip, *Piva Yoke*, was ready for sorties on 9 January 1944. (*NARA*)

Three US Navy Scout Bomber Douglas (SBD) dive-bombers fly in formation over Mt Bagana as they head southwards after a bombing raid on Kavieng on the north-western tip of New Ireland north of Rabaul in the Bismarck Archipelago. Heavy bombers alone, like the B-24s and B-17s based on Guadalcanal and in the New Hebrides had been unable to destroy Rabaul. Medium dive-bombers and torpedo bombers of the US Navy and Marine Air Wing would have to be used, as shown above. However, these actions required the bomber strip near the Piva River, *Piva Uncle*, to be completed first. Additionally, the twin-engined USAAF B-25 'Mitchell' and A-20 'Havoc' medium bombers based on New Guinea would also contribute to the neutralization of Rabaul. *(NARA)*

Chapter Five

Japanese Counter-Attack and Perimeter Defence, March 1944

It would now become Griswold's turn to defend the perimeter and his newly functioning airfields from the Japanese as General Hyakutake was making preparations for an all-out offensive scheduled for early March 1944.

Hyakutake was going to attack primarily with the IJA 6th Division, commanded by Kanda, and elements of the 17th Army. Even after moving his headquarters opposite the American perimeter and in possession of high ground to directly observe it, Hyakutake would be yet another senior Japanese commander who was going to underestimate the strength of the opposing American forces, believing that there were only 20,000 US Army troops at Torokina. However, the 17th Army commander was to embark on an all-out assault on the XIVth Corps perimeter without much air support, since most of the Japanese aircraft and surface carriers had been withdrawn from the Solomon Islands. The Japanese still believed at this late date that if the American position on Bougainville could be captured, Rabaul's neutralization, facilitated by the three Allied airfields at Torokina, could be overcome, allowing that New Britain Island bastion to once again play an integral part in the South Pacific War. Nonetheless, Hyakutake did amass well over 15,000 infantry and artillery troops, the latter manning 75mm pack Howitzers, and 105mm and 150mm guns, which were hauled onto ridges dominating the perimeter, to hurl against the American perimeter, which was the greatest concentration of IJA forces that would fight in the South Pacific. The reason why it was not larger was that he had to retain the remaining 18,000 troops of the 17th Army to hold the rest of Bougainville's northern and southern ends at Buka and Buin respectively.

The term perimeter for the XIVth Corps' 23,000 yard defensive zone underestimates how it bristled with mortar pits, pillboxes, trenches and rifle pits with clear fields of fire and reserve positions in depth. XIVth Corps' array of artillery was also impressive with pre-registered 75mm pack Howitzer companies, along with 155mm and 105mm Howitzer battalions and 150mm 'Long Tom' cannon and 90mm AA batteries to hail HE shells on Japanese concentration areas. From the perimeter's left, south of the Laruma River, to its right, just astride the Torokina River, the XIVth Corps' regiments were arrayed as follows: 148th, 129th and 145th of the 37th Division moving onto the 164th, 182nd and 132nd of the Americal Division. The fighter strip was on the beach at Cape Torokina within the Americal Division's perimeter zone, while *Piva Yoke* and *Piva Uncle* were in the 37th Division's half. Additionally, XIVth Corps had attached to it the 1st Battalion of the Fiji Infantry Regiment, which gathered vital intelligence of the Japanese build-up while scouting inland in the jungle.

General Kanda, the IJA 6th Division commander, organized his troops into three separate units, each one named for its commander. The Japanese infantrymen possessed just two weeks of rations, since it was believed that the Americans would be defeated within that time-frame. After Japanese infiltrators began cutting the bands of American concertina wire on 7 March 1944, a massive enemy artillery bombardment, the largest in the Pacific War up until then, erupted at dawn the following day, targeting the Piva airfields from the northern and eastern sides of the perimeter, necessitating evacuation of the Allied aircraft to Munda on New Georgia.

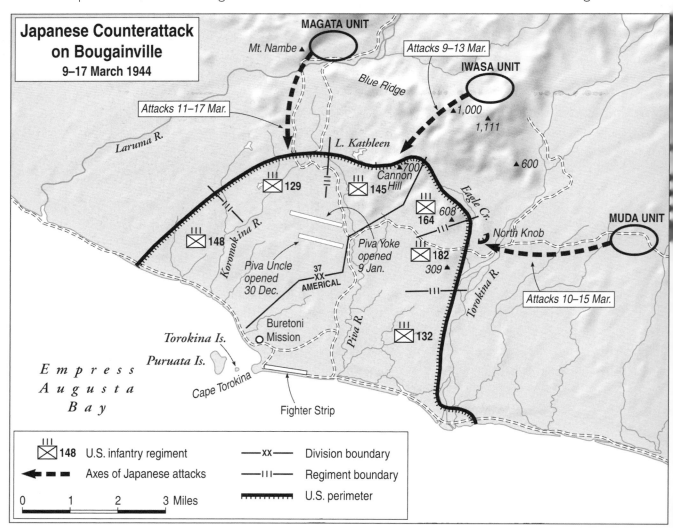

The Americans responded with an intense and accurate counter-battery fire on the Japanese Howitzer positions. It was now time for the usual uncoordinated enemy infantry assault by different units on the American perimeter.

Japanese infantry under Major General Shun Iwasa (the Iwasa Unit), began the attack first after midnight on 9 March, heading southwards towards the centre of the perimeter to scale the steep slopes of Hill 700. This force numbered over 4,000 troops, elements of which were from the 23rd and 13th Infantry Regiments. Its mission, after penetrating the American 145th Infantry Regiment's area, under Colonel Cecil Whitcomb, within the 37th Division's half of the perimeter, was to seize the two airfields, *Piva Yoke* and *Piva Uncle*. Small units of Japanese infantry were able to blast through the wire with bangalore torpedoes, seizing several American pillboxes during the early morning hours, creating a 150-yard wide penetration that the 37th Division's commanding general, Beightler, rapidly responded to. Companies from the division's reserve, the 1st Battalion/145th Infantry Regiment, eventually reoccupied most of the previously over-run pillboxes. On 10 March, after bitter close-action combat, further American counter-attacks by the 1st and 2nd Battalions/ 145th Infantry Regiment reduced the extent of the enemy salient considerably. As dawn broke on 11 March, Iwasa launched a futile, hour-long, battalion-sized *banzai* charge up the Hill 700's steep slope, with horrific casualties suffered by the enemy, largely due to 37mm canister fire into their massed formation. Iwasa withdrew his battered force 2 miles from the battlefield on 12 March, after the 2nd Battalion/

Map 5. By March 1944, Japanese 17th Army commander Lieutenant General Hyakutake assembled a counter-attacking force to move across the mountains and pierce Major General Oscar W. Griswold's US Army XIVth Corps (37th and Americal Divisions) 23,000-yard perimeter replete with prepared defences and manned by six veteran army regiments. The Japanese goal was the seizure of the American airfields, *Piva Uncle* and *Piva Yoke*, opened on 30 December 1943 and 9 January 1944 respectively. However, the Japanese attacked in a dispersed and unsupported manner. Early on 9 March, elements of the Iwasa Unit attacked Hill 700, which was the initial Japanese target at the eastern end of the 145th Infantry's sector. The western border of this US Army regiment's position was near Lake Kathleen. For the next four days the 145th Regiment reduced the Iwasa Unit's penetration and, as such, prevented a major Japanese exploitation of the northernmost point of the perimeter. During the early hours of 10 March, the Muda Unit threatened to overwhelm a 182nd Infantry position on Hill 260 (North Knob), which was a geographically isolated outpost sticking out of the American perimeter. Repeated attacks by the Americans to retake this position failed until massive XIVth Corps fire-power compelled the Japanese to retreat into the jungle. The third Japanese axis of attack was made by the Magata Unit on 11 March against the 129th Infantry's 3,900-yard position west of Hill 700 among some lowland creeks. Despite strong American defences and clear fields of fire, three Japanese battalions made a 100-yard penetration of the perimeter during the pre-dawn hours of 15 March, which was reversed by an American tank–infantry counter-attack. After all three axes of Japanese attacks failed the surviving elements of the Iwasa, Muda and Magata Units regrouped in the Bougainville jungle for a last surge onto the 129th Infantry's position in the middle of the 37th Division's portion of the perimeter. After a minor Japanese penetration during darkness on 23 March, American artillery, heavy mortar bombardment and a tank-infantry attack by the 129th Infantry decimated the enemy in front of the American perimeter. The Japanese withdrew the following afternoon after suffering horrific losses. (*Philip Schwartzberg, Meridian Mapping*)

148th Infantry Regiment eliminated the entire enemy salient as well as recovered enemy dispositions and plans for the entire counter-offensive from the corpse of a Japanese officer.

On 10 March, Colonel Toyoharei Muda's unit of over 1,300 infantry from the remainder of the 13th Infantry Regiment plus engineers was assigned to attack Hill 260 in front of the American 182nd Infantry Regiment, under Colonel William Long, of the Americal Division. The Japanese commanders had planned that after penetrating the XIVth Corps perimeter, the Muda Unit was to serve as the larger Iwasa Unit's left flank protection. The Japanese sent in two companies of their 13th Infantry Regiment onto the South Knob of the hill, which captured an observation post atop a 150-foot tree from eighty Americans of an artillery observation unit, sending the GIs fleeing to the North Knob. For two days, elements of the American 182nd Infantry Regiment tried to regain the South Knob to no avail. On 12 March, called 'Bloody Sunday' by the Americal Division, elements of the 182nd Infantry Regiment unsuccessfully assaulted the Japanese positions of the South Knob from the west and northwest. The troops of the Americal Division sparred with the enemy occupants on the South Knob for an additional three days, until Griswold broke off the attacks, realizing that the enemy could not threaten his perimeter in their current strength. The 150-foot banyan tree finally fell to American artillery fire on 17 March.

Hyakutake's complex plan envisioned that XIVth Corps would commit its reserves to staunch perimeter penetrations by both the Iwasa and Muda Units on 9 and 10 March respectively. However, with foreknowledge of the Japanese plan, Beightler avoided depletion of his troop strength from the next intended Japanese attack point on the American perimeter. Awareness of the Japanese artillery dispositions from the captured documents was to aid the accuracy of XIVth Corps' own artillery fire missions immensely. At dawn on 12 March, a 4,300 attack force, the Magata Unit, named after its commander Colonel Isashi Magata, supported by artillery and mortar barrages, comprised mostly of Japanese infantrymen from the reinforced IJA 45th Infantry Regiment, would be hurled down a logging trail that paralleled the Numa Numa Trail at the American 129th Infantry Regiment in the 37th Division's sector of the perimeter, west of Hill 700, which was low ground. Hyakutake's plan called for the convergence of the Iwasa and Magata Units, after their respective breakthroughs, to capture the two Piva airfields. Then, all three units were to combine and drive south to the fighter strip on the beach at Cape Torokina.

The Magata Unit attacked along a 100-yard front against Beightler's 2nd Battalion/129th Infantry Regiment in the centre of the 37th Division's perimeter. The Japanese had broken through an initial defence line and took some American pillboxes before a counter-attack by C and G Companies of the 1st Battalion/129th Infantry Regiment, acting as a reserve, reclaimed a few of the positions and stopped another enemy assault later that day. At dawn on 13 March, the Japanese struck again, but Beightler personally responded with Sherman tanks from XIVth Corps reserve and, along with his infantry, his original lines were restored. For his personal combat leadership at the Front, Beightler was awarded a Silver Star. Pre-dawn Japanese attacks on both 15 and 17 March made modest inroads into the 37th Division's perimeter. After a four-day lull in Japanese assaults from 18–22 March, Magata put together a force of almost 5,000 infantry after amalgamating elements of the Iwasa and Muda Units to replace his own 45th Regiment's casualties. Magata mounted an attack late on 23 March against the American's 129th Infantry Regiment's perimeter sector where Cox Creek abuts it. However, the Americans were again forewarned after intercepting a wireless communication sent from 17th Army Headquarters to Tokyo, which pinpointed the time and place of the attack. After a small Japanese penetration, in proximity to the 2nd Battalion/129th Infantry Regiment's command post, Beightler counter-attacked on the morning of 24 March with infantry, tanks and anti-tank guns. By noon, the enemy salient was reduced. As the Japanese retreated, XIVth Corps artillery, on Beightler's request, rained down almost 15,000 rounds on enemy troops.

The Japanese counter-offensive was defeated. Hyakutake requested and received permission from General Imamura, Commanding General, IJA 8th Area Army, to withdraw, and so the enemy began its retreat on 28 March. The Iwasa and Muda Units withdrew south to Buin, while Magata's 1,500 survivors went north via the Numa Numa Trail. Battlefield estimates listed the Japanese casualties at over 8,500 killed and wounded during the nineteen-day enemy counter-offensive. However, after-action estimates by the IJA 8th Area Army headquarters placed their casualty figures at over 12,000 killed and wounded. As a testimony to the Americans' fortified positions, interior lines and skilled direction of reserves, tanks and artillery, the dead among the XIVth Corps casualties were much less than the enemy's, at 263. If not for the National Guardsmen of the 37th and Americal Divisions in this largely forgotten northern Solomon Island conflict, as Admiral Morison wrote, as part of his massive opus, 'Kanda's [6th IJA Division] forces could have captured the Perimeter and the Torokina airdrome, wiping out the gains of the Bougainville campaign and raising new hopes at Rabaul, but not for the stern resistance offered by the infantry and artillery of the XIVth Corps.'

As for the Japanese, their commanders, after the failed March 1944 counter-offensive against the XIVth Corps, admitted defeat and retreated to the east and south, from which no further Imperial offensives would be launched. There, the once-mighty 17th Army would be isolated and have to resort to planting crops and gardens for subsistence, while the American forces, within a slightly enlarged perimeter, simply patrolled aggressively and contained them in a 'vast jungle prison camp'.

(**Above**) Major General Oscar W. Griswold (*left*), the XIVth Corps Commander on Bougainville, along with Major General Robert S. Beightler, Commanding General 37th Infantry Division (*right*). Both generals contributed greatly to the reinvigoration of the stalled offensive on Munda during the New Georgia campaign in July–August 1943. Griswold would command both the 37th and the Americal Divisions, the latter under the 43rd Division's former commanding general, Major General John R. Hodge, who arrived on Bougainville on 28 December 1943 to take over the eastern sector of the perimeter from the 3rd Marines. (*NARA*)

(**Opposite page**) Soldiers from the 37th Infantry Division march to the front lines through the thick mud characterizing the jungle inland from the landing beaches at Torokina. The 148th Infantry Regiment of this Ohio National Guard Division, under Major General Robert S. Beightler, landed on 9 November 1943. Within two weeks, the 37th Division's artillery, along with its 129th and 145th Regiments, would also land. (*NARA*)

(**Opposite above**) Army soldiers that recently landed on Bougainville had to contend with the same mud inland from the Torokina beaches as the Marines did earlier. Here, a 2.5-ton truck loaded with supplies and hauling a cart behind it moves over some wire matting to facilitate getting to the front lines. Note, a rifle is lying on the hood of the truck and extends into the cab should the driver come under enemy sniper fire due to the incessant Japanese practice of infiltration. (*USAMHI*)

(**Opposite below**) Soldiers of the 37th Division walk along a coastal tidal pool carrying belts of ammunition and other supplies to a perimeter machine-gun outpost as the army took over Marine positions in late December 1943. (*NARA*)

(**Above**) On Christmas Day 1943, the initial troops of the Americal Division, the 164th Regimental Combat Team (RCT) arrived from the Fiji Islands to relieve the combat-worn 3rd Marines, who had been in action for seven weeks. This was a repeat performance by this regiment as they had previously provided desperately needed reinforcements for the Marines defending Henderson Field during the Guadalcanal campaign. The 182nd RCT of the Americal Division arrived with the division's commanding general on 28 December to take over the perimeter from the 21st Marines. On 9 February 1944, the Americal's 132nd RCT arrived and joined the perimeter defence. (*NARA*)

(**Opposite above**) Soldiers of the Americal Division move forward in single-file through some partially cleared thick brush to reconnoitre for any enemy positions. Until mid-December, the Japanese had used the surrounding high ground atop the Torokina landing beaches to shell the beachhead and the newly operational fighter strip along the coast. (*NARA*)

(**Above**) Two GIs in a sandbag-reinforced foxhole covered with a canvas tent half-sheet man their 0.30-inch calibre Browning light machine-gun covering a trail near the Laruma River to the western side of the perimeter. (*NARA*)

(**Opposite below**) In early March, Staff Sergeant Frank Ritter, of an anti-tank company in the 129th Infantry Regiment of the 37th Division, fires his carbine from a prepared position at Japanese snipers. The barrel of his 37mm anti-tank gun extends through the embrasure of his log-fortified entrenchment. Within days, the enemy would launch their massive counter-attack against the Army's XIVth Corps perimeter. Once again, the 37mm anti-tank gun, firing canister like a 'giant shotgun' at Japanese massed troop concentrations, would be an excellent defensive weapon for the American infantry. (*NARA*)

(**Above**) A soldier lines up his rifle in a sandbag-fortified foxhole called 'Sniper Inn' along the perimeter with a camouflaged tent half-sheet as cover at the end of March after the successful XIVth Corps perimeter defence against the Japanese counter-attack. (*USAMHI*)

(**Opposite above**) Two soldiers from the 37th Infantry Division sit at the ready at a lean-to outpost. Their rifles and helmets are in the immediate vicinity if enemy infiltration becomes apparent. The soldier on the left is on the telephone, so this may have been a mortar or light artillery position receiving coordinates for a fire mission. (*NARA*)

(**Opposite below**) A 60mm mortar crew of the 37th Division's 145th Infantry Regiment fires a round from their sandbagged emplacement on Hill 700 on 15 February 1944. The soldier on the left is holding a 'walkie-talkie' in his right hand to get fire directions. This elevated site was the far right of the 37th Division's perimeter defence, which extended from Empress Augusta Bay west of the Koromokina Lagoon arcing north-west to Hill 700. The Americal Division's line ran from just east of Hill 700, where the 164th Infantry Regiment's left flank tied in with the 145th's right. The sector of the perimeter occupied by the rest of the Americal Division's 182nd and 132nd Infantry Regiments ran along the west bank of the Torokina River to Empress Augusta Bay. (*NARA*)

Soldiers of the 37th Division's 145th Infantry Regiment carry water to the crest of the hill, to their outpost positions in February 1944. Hill 700 had been a site of earlier fierce combat between the Marines and the Japanese, the latter having utilized this position to shell the Torokina beachhead. Now, the 145th, on the extreme right of the 37th Division, was charged with holding Hill 700, just over a mile to the west of Lake Kathleen, as it was the highest point possessed by the Americans. (*USAMHI*)

(**Opposite above**) A trio of American soldiers, ever alert for enemy infiltrators, passes by the bitterly contested base of Hill 700 on 8 March 1944 just prior to the Japanese counter-attack. The Japanese 'Iwasa Unit' attacked the 145th Regiment's perimeter along a vector between Lake Kathleen and Hill 700 from 9 to 13 March. The Iwasa Unit, named for its commander Major General Shun Iwasa, comprised about 4,000 troops from the IJA 23rd and 13th Infantry Regiments. The three GIs carry their M1 semi-automatic rifles at the ready as they move through the mud at the hill's base. (*USAMHI*)

(**Opposite below**) Two soldiers man their 60mm M2 mortar and demonstrate their determination to assist their infantrymen in holding on to the American perimeter at Hill 260 or North Knob during the March 1944 enemy counter-attack. These mortars, held at the company level, could deliver explosive, smoke and illumination rounds at a rate of fire of about twenty rounds per minute. Hill 260 was attacked by the 'Muda Unit' in front of the Americal Division's 182nd Infantry Regiment near its junction with the right flank of its sister regiment, the 164th, on 10–15 March. Colonel Toyoharei Muda's unit comprised over 1,300 infantry from the remainder of the IJA's 13th Infantry Regiment, plus Japanese engineers. (*NARA*)

(**Above**) An American 81mm M1 mortar crew fires a round across the Tainamutu River onto a Japanese position near Kuraio Mission, to the east of the American perimeter's left flank. Depending on the weight of the mortar round used, the maximum range for this weapon was between 1,300–3,300 yards and was equivalent in explosive force to a shell from either a 75mm or 105mm Howitzer. The 81mm mortar was the most powerful weapon the infantry battalion commander had under his direct control. (*NARA*)

(**Opposite above**) A crew from a chemical battalion fires rounds from a 4.2 inch chemical mortar. This weapon was derived from the First World War vintage British Stokes mortar. Rounds are stacked to the right of the mortar tube. This weapon first saw action with the US Army in Sicily in July 1943. The minimum charge could be lobbed about 350 yards. However, by adding more disks onto the cartridge container of the shell, this distance could be extended to about 4,500 yards. (*USAMHI*)

(**Opposite below**) A gunner fires his M8 75mm pack Howitzer, point-blank through the embrasure of the sandbagged emplacement, as indicated by the completely depressed barrel, at Japanese positions attacking Hill 260 or North Knob on 10–15 March 1944 on the right flank of XIVth Corps perimeter in the America's 182nd Regiment's sector. The M8 75mm pack Howitzer was devastating in breaking-up enemy infantry formations, as was evidenced in the combat against the 'Muda Unit' at Hill 260. (*NARA*)

(**Opposite above**) A column of American infantry marches past a trio of M4 Sherman tanks down a road built by Navy 'Seabees' before the army arrived. Coordinated tactics between armour and escorting infantry was perfected on New Georgia by General Griswold after he took over the New Georgia Occupation Force to expedite the drive onto Munda Airfield in August 1943. (*NARA*)

(**Opposite below**) African-American gunners of Section 2, Battery B, 49th Coast Artillery ram a round through the breech of a 155mm 'Long Tom' cannon under its camouflage netting on Bougainville in April 1944. The Long Tom was one of the most important weapons in the US Army's long-range artillery inventory during the Second World War and, interestingly, was based on a French design used during the First World War. Design to implementation into service took over a decade for the US Army. It had a maximum range of over 25,000 yards and fired one 200lb round per minute. (*NARA*)

(**Above**) Soldiers from the 2nd Battalion, 25th Infantry Regimental Combat Team (RCT) of the 93rd Division (Colored) carry mortar shells across a waterway on Bougainville roughly 500 yards away from where elements of the Japanese 17th Army were holed up in late March–early April 1944 after the enemy's failed counter-attack on the American perimeter. (*USAMHI*)

Soldiers from the 37th Infantry Division advance through shellfire-destroyed banyan trees in pursuit of the retreating Japanese after their attempt to break through the XIVth Corps' left flank and attack the *Piva Uncle* and *Piva Yoke* airfields in March 1944. *(NARA)*

(**Opposite above**) African-American soldiers of Company E, 25th Regimental Combat Team (RCT) of the 93rd Division (Colored) clean their dissembled M1 Garand semi-automatic rifles in a bivouac along the East–West Trail on Bougainville in early April 1944. These troops had fanned out from the American perimeter to pursue the retreating Japanese as well as enlarge the recently defended perimeter and establish trail blocks. These actions were also to give combat experience to the elements of the 93rd Division (Colored), who arrived on Bougainville in late March after the failed Japanese counter-attack on the American perimeter. *(NARA)*

(**Opposite below**) In mid-April 1944, an African–American artillery crew load and prepare to fire a 105mm Howitzer in support of infantry operations pursuing the Japanese after the enemy's failed March counter-attack. This crew was from Section 1, Battery A, 593rd Field Artillery Battalion attached to the 93rd Division (Colored). *(NARA)*

American Division soldiers charge uphill across the trunks of banyan trees onto Japanese positions during the third week of March 1944 after the 'Muda Unit' abandoned its attack on the XIVth Corps perimeter in the vicinity of Hill 260 or North Knob. (*NARA*)

(**Opposite above**) Soldiers of the 182nd Infantry Regiment of the American Division, which formed the right flank of the XIVth Corps perimeter, ascend the North Knob of Hill 260 in pursuit of retreating Japanese from the 'Muda Unit' during the third week of March 1944. The GIs are armed with flame-throwers, rifles and bazookas and often engaged in hand-to-hand combat to wrest control of the enemy dug-outs on the face of the hill. (*NARA*)

(**Opposite below**) Moving westward from the left flank of the XIVth Corps perimeter, soldiers from the 37th Division move through dense chest-deep swampy jungle in the vicinity of the Kuraio Mission in pursuit of the retreating enemy during late March 1944. (*NARA*)

(**Opposite above**) During a fire-fight against retreating Japanese infantry, American soldiers lie prone and fire the M1 Garand semi-automatic rifles at the enemy at the edge of the jungle. (*NARA*)

(**Above**) An American soldier fires his M1 Garand semi-automatic rifle at Japanese infantrymen in concealed ground dug-outs or 'spider holes' in early March 1944. After the soldier expended eight rounds from his M1, the stripper-clip ejected from the internal magazine of the rifle would make a distinctive pinging sound that could often betray the GI's position in dense jungle, such as shown. A skilled rifleman could fire forty to fifty rounds per minute from this stable gun platform with relatively low recoil, giving this weapon the distinction of the highest sustained rate of fire of any standard-issue rifle during the war. It had an effective range of over 450 yards. However, it did have a considerable weight of 9.6lb (unloaded) as a disadvantage, especially for jungle combat. (*USAMHI*)

(**Opposite below**) An American soldier tosses his standard Mk II 'pineapple' fragmentation hand-grenade at a Japanese pillbox during the Japanese counter-attack of March 1944. At 3.5 inches in length, the hand grenade packed roughly 2 ounces of explosive charge and had a total weight of 1.3lb. The serrated 'pineapple' configuration was to maximize grip for the grenade-hurler. The soldier crouching to the right is holding his Browning automatic rifle (BAR). (*USAMHI*)

(**Above**) Two GIs charge forward under suppressive fire from one of their machine-gun-crews to rush a Japanese position. The soldier on the right is holding his M1 Carbine rifle, while the one on the left is armed with an M1897 Winchester pump shotgun. This shotgun was designed by John Browning and over 1,000,000 were manufactured from 1897–1957. It had a 5-round tubular magazine and was chambered for either 12- or 16-gauge. It was labelled as a 'Trench Gun' during the First World War, having an effective firing range of roughly 22 yards. For close action combat an adapter with a bayonet lug for affixing a M1917 bayonet could also be used. (*USAMHI*)

(**Opposite above**) An American soldier leads from the point of a patrol with a flame-thrower team and accompanying infantrymen. The group is searching out enemy pillboxes and dug-outs that are offering stubborn resistance. The flame-thrower was feared by the Japanese, who had resorted to a suicidal defence in their bunkers, and became available to the South Pacific Force in late 1943. (*NARA*)

(**Opposite below**) A plume of flame is emitted from a flame-thrower in the upper left background as fellow infantrymen lay suppressive fire down on a fortified Japanese position. The flame-thrower had a limited range of up to a maximum of 130 feet, thus the need to get close with infantry support. The device was heavy at almost 70lb filled with a fuel capacity of 4 gallons. (*USAMHI*)

(**Opposite above**) A squad of infantrymen with fixed bayonets crouch down behind an M4 Sherman medium tank as heavier American armour was employed against the retreating Japanese after the failed March 1944 counter-attack. The XIVth Corps commanding general had first employed Marine Defence Battalion M3 Stuart light tanks with accompanying infantry on New Georgia while besieging Munda in the summer of 1943. (*NARA*)

(**Opposite below**) In this now iconic photograph, an M4 Sherman medium tank of the 754th Tank Battalion, called *Lucky Legs II*, advances against the retreating Japanese in mid- to late March 1944, with American infantrymen from the 37th Division's 129th Regiment in close support providing rifle fire to keep the suicidal Japanese from rushing the tank with explosives or grenades. (*USAMHI*)

(**Above**) A close-up view of the terrain that the M4 Sherman medium tank had to traverse in order to close with the retreating Japanese is shown. Accompanying infantrymen from the 129th Regiment, 37th Division, move warily behind the armour in ferreting out the hiding enemy on 16 March 1944. In contrast to the Marines' M3 light tanks on New Georgia, the Army's M4 medium tanks had a more powerful 75mm turret gun as well as thicker armour. (*USAMHI*)

(**Above**) Army infantrymen ascend rugged vegetation behind an M4 Sherman medium tank in pursuit of the Japanese east of the perimeter. This Bougainville terrain was marked by a number of strategic hills of various heights. (*NARA*)

(**Opposite above**) Soldiers from the 129th Infantry Regiment, 37th Division mop up sequestered Japanese positions outside the XIVth Corps perimeter on 16 March 1944. A pair of M4 Sherman medium tanks is visible in the left background. (*NARA*)

(**Opposite below**) The human cost of a successful defence against the Japanese counter-attack of March 1944, as the bodies of dead American infantrymen are carried out of the jungle outposts of Hill 700 on litters to be taken to the rear by an open armoured vehicle for identification and burial on 13 March 1944. XIVth Corps suffered 263 dead during the perimeter's defence. (*NARA*)

(**Opposite above**) On 17 March 1944, Private First Class Emil Raths, a flame-thrower from a headquarters company of the 2nd Battalion, 129th Infantry Regiment, 37th Division peers in through the aperture of a Japanese pillbox soon after ten Japanese infantrymen chose death by fiery means rather than surrender. (*NARA*)

(**Opposite below**) The wooded Bougainville terrain on the perimeter of Company F, 129th Infantry Regiment, 37th Division is littered with the corpses of dead Japanese infantrymen of the 'Magata Unit' during their failed attack on 16 March 1944. The 'hob-nailed' appearance on the soles of the Japanese soldiers' boots is shown in the right foreground. (*NARA*)

(**Above**) A dead Japanese infantryman clutches a machine-gun ammunition clip as he lies in a rifle pit on 13 March 1944. Battlefield estimates placed the Japanese casualties at 5,000 men killed and over 3,000 wounded in its attempt to pierce the XIVth Corps perimeter and seize the airfields within it in their counter-offensive spanning from 9–17 March 1944. After-action Japanese 8th Army Headquarters casualty estimates for the IJA 6th Division and elements of the 17th Army were considerably higher. (*NARA*)

Japanese soldier from the 'Magata Unit' lies dead in a foxhole with a machine-gun ammunition clip nearby, close to the Company F, 129th Infantry Regiment, 37th Division's sector of the XIVth Corps' perimeter on 19 March 1944. (NARA)

One of the few surviving Japanese taken as prisoner after the failed counter-attack is given food by his American captors as he holds a fork in his right hand. Customarily, Japanese prisoners were stripped of almost or all of their clothing, since bitter experience during earlier Solomon Island campaigns demonstrated that the captive enemy would often set-off hand-grenades rather than fail their bushido code. (USAMHI)

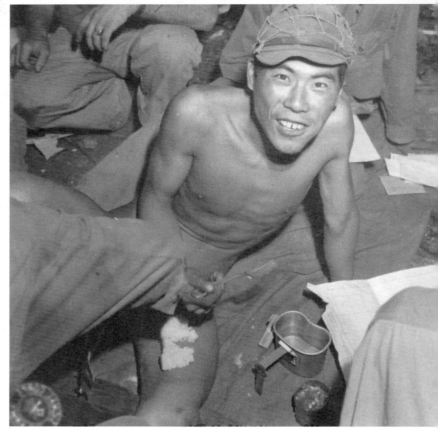

Chapter Six

Australian Action on Bougainville, November 1944–August 1945

Until mid-1943, the majority of MacArthur's land forces in SWPA were Australian, but during the latter part of the year American soldiers began to outnumber them. In mid-July 1944, MacArthur sent a memorandum to Blamey informing him that Australian troops would relieve American forces in the northern Solomon Islands, as well as on New Guinea and New Britain, in order for the Americans to participate in the upcoming Philippine Island invasions.

MacArthur did not specify to Blamey how to neutralize the Japanese on New Guinea and in the northern Solomons Islands, most notably on Bougainville. Blamey, as Allied Land Forces Commander, SWPA, in specific charge of the AIF, had some latitude in conducting offensive operations. His decision was to wage a controlled offensive to wear down the Japanese in short, sporadic battles, while maintaining Australian casualties to a minimum. On 18 October 1944, Blamey issued Operational Order No. 66, 'offensive action to destroy enemy resistance as opportunity offers without committing major forces'. After the failed counter-offensive against the American perimeter at Cape Torokina in March 1944, the Japanese had not withered. Rather they were isolated, but self-sufficient, thus remaining a formidable fighting force. Blamey did not intend for the Australian soldiers to be 'edged out at the end' of combat glory against the Japanese.

As a result of Blamey's memorandum, Lieutenant General Vernon A.H. Sturdee, the First Australian Army General Officer Commanding (GOC), responsible for New Guinea and Bougainville, issued his instructions on 13 November 1944. Sturdee wanted 2nd Australian Corps, under Lieutenant General Stanley George Savige, to continue its relief of the American forces on Bougainville and the Outer Islands and to neutralize the Japanese by vigorous patrolling and harassing action in order to ascertain the enemy's strength, so that later major offensive plans could be made to destroy the remaining Japanese units.

From September–October 1944, the initial landings of Australian support units and combat troops at the Torokina beachhead occurred. A lack of shipping would delay the relief of the entire US XIVth Corps, under Griswold. On 22 November, the 2nd Australian Corps assumed command of the northern Solomon Islands area from US XIVth Corps, with the 3rd Australian Division relieving the US Americal and 37th Infantry Divisions in succession on Bougainville. The Australian 11th and 29th Infantry Brigades would not arrive until mid-December 1944. As the Australian 2nd Corps set up their Torokina perimeter headquarters, the staff there had under-estimated the Japanese strength on Bougainville at approximately 18,000 troops. There were really many more throughout the island, which outnumbered the Australian 3rd Division and the attached two independent brigades.

The Australian objectives began in Bougainville's Central Sector, which was to clear the enemy from the high ground, Pearl Ridge. This height dominated the high ground of the Emperor Mountain Range in Central Bougainville. By so doing, the Australians would be able to completely protect the route to Torokina and to look down on the Japanese base at Numa Numa. The capture of Pearl Ridge would also mitigate any large-scale enemy movement between the northern and southern ends of Bougainville, from Buka to Buin, by controlling this position between Numa Numa and Kieta, as this crest would enable the Australians an unencumbered view of the east coast of the island. The Japanese had reinforced Pearl Ridge with pillboxes occupied by over 500 infantrymen, since this locale was where three main east–west trails across Bougainville intersected one another. Additionally, the Japanese numbered approximately 2,000 troops at Numa Numa, comprising the 38th Independent Mixed Brigade, with the 81st Infantry Regiment as a nucleus. These enemy troops would be reinforced by another 1,500 infantrymen as the Japanese anticipated an Australian move towards the island's east coast.

In late November 1944, elements of the Australian 7th Infantry Brigade began intensive patrolling to reconnoitre Japanese positions and trail conditions. Engineers began upgrading Numa Numa Trail into a Jeep track. On 29–30 November, the Australian 9th Infantry Battalion attacked Little George Hill in the Piaterapaia area of Bougainville's Central sector. This marked the Australians' combat debut on the island. This was followed by an assault against the Japanese entrenched position on Artillery Hill and the continued drive to Pearl Ridge. The Australian offensive into the Central Sector of Bougainville never reached the island's east coast as planned. Thus the island was not severed into isolated northern and southern halves. However, much of the high ground between the two mountain ranges was seized such that both sides of Bougainville were visible to the Australians

In Bougainville's Northern Sector, the Australians planned to force the Japanese garrison into the narrow Bonis Peninsula. From 20 January to 9 February 1945, elements of the Australian 11th Infantry Brigade began pushing north along

Bougainville's western coast and confronted elements of the Japanese 38th Independent Mixed Brigade (IMB) on Tsimba Ridge, a half-mile south of the Genga River. By the end of March 1945, the Australians cleared the Soraken Peninsula in Bougainville's Northern sector, well to the north of Tsimba Ridge. This offensive into the Northern Sector was successful as it moved up the west coast of Bougainville, except for the failed and aborted amphibious landing at the Porton Plantation on 7–8 June 1945. The landing there was fiercely repelled by entrenched Japanese, who were quickly reinforced, necessitating an Australian withdrawal. This constituted one of the few defeats for the Australians on Bougainville and effectively stopped the Australian northern advance, due to casualties incurred in that sector.

However, the main Japanese troop concentrations were in the Southern Sector of the island. It was here that the decisive Australian campaign battles were to be fought to destroy the enemy forces on Bougainville emanating from their main installation at Buin.

In December 1944, south of the Torokina River and along the Buin Road area, the Australians started to clear the swampy area south of the Jaba River and push forward to the Puriata River. On 26 March 1945, at Slater's Knoll, the Australian 25th Battalion encountered intensified Japanese activity in the area. After nightfall, while under a full moon, the Japanese attacked the Australian's perimeter in massed infantry charges. The following morning brought Japanese infiltration and small-scale attacks as Slater's Knoll became besieged with an inability to evacuate wounded Australians. The early morning of 29 March also heralded new Japanese bayonet charges against Australian rifle and weapons pits, which continued throughout the day. The following day, the Japanese continued their attacks with infantry and grenade discharger shelling of Australian positions. Notably on that day, four Matilda Infantry ('I') tanks of B Squadron, 2/4th Armoured Regiment were coming across the Puriata to the aid of the 25th Battalion. Without the appearance of Australian tanks on the battlefield at Slater's Knoll, the battalion could have been overrun.

During May–June 1945, the Australian 15th Infantry Brigade pushed further south across the Puriata River with one battalion on the Buin Rd and a second one on the Commando Road, while a third was held in reserve. However, by July 1945, this southward advance towards Buin was halted at the Mivo River by monsoon rains and flooding. Within a matter of weeks the war with Japan would end.

Australian troops of the 9th Infantry Battalion, 7th Brigade cross the Laruma River at a ford as it parallels the southern portion of the Numa Numa Trail to move into the vicinity of Piaterapaia and Little George Hill, in order to relieve the American 2nd Battalion, 132nd Infantry Regiment, Americal Division on 23 November 1944. Just hours prior to this movement, Lieutenant General Savige, General Officer Commanding (GOC) Australian 2nd Corps assumed command of operations in the Northern Solomons from General Griswold's American XIVth Corps. Savige wanted the 9th Battalion to move beyond the immediate Torokina perimeter into the mountains north of the Doiabi River, to block the overland approach to Torokina at the southern terminus of the Numa Numa Trail, between the Emperor and Crown Prince Mountain Ranges. In addition to protecting the perimeter, the Australians were to harass the Japanese with aggressive patrolling. (*AWM*)

On 29 November 1944, men of D Company, 9th Infantry Battalion start immediately digging themselves into a defensive position that they just captured from the Japanese on Little George Hill and prepare for the inevitable enemy counter-attack. The Australian to the left is holding the characteristic Owen gun that was produced in Australia as he looks over the dead bodies of Japanese troops who had previously occupied the position. The Owen gun had proved to be rugged and reliable in the muddy and harsh terrain of both Bougainville and New Guinea. While the men of D Company killed roughly twenty Japanese in their pillboxes, several Australians would become the first casualties of their campaign. In the Central Sector of Bougainville, the Australians identified the capture of the roughly 2,800-foot Pearl Ridge, which was the crest of the Emperor Range astride the Numa Numa Trail, as a first priority to block the enemy's eastern approach to the Torokina perimeter from the locales of Numa Numa and Kieta. The capture of Little George Hill heralded the opening of the Australian campaign on Bougainville. Japanese Lieutenant General Hyakutake Harukichi, the 17th Army commander, did not believe that the Australians would advance eastward using an overland route from their perimeter and, if they did, it would not be for at least two months after relieving the Americans. (AWM)

(**Opposite page**) Australian troops work hard to get through chest-deep swamp water in January 1945 in the Southern Sector. The Australians are wearing their new green jungle berets. Japanese Lieutenant General Hyakutake Harukichi, the 17th Army commander, did not think that the Australians would advance from Torokina through the swamps and rugged hilly terrain. Campaigning in this area for the Australians became known as the 'Battle of the Swamps', with the wet terrain referred to as 'black slime'. The infantryman in the foreground has an Owen Machine Carbine commonly referred to as an Owen gun. This weapon was developed and named after its designer, Evelyn Ernest Owen, a young tinkerer without any formal engineering or gunsmith training. After many bureaucratic hurdles and rigorous field-testing and comparisons, the Owen gun was manufactured at the Lysaght Newcastle Steelworks, a metal fabrication firm located at Port Kembla in New South Wales, Australia, reaching front line troops by early 1943. The majority of the 50,000 Owen guns were deployed in the Pacific. The gun fired a 9mm (.35 inch) calibre Parabellum bullet and had an overall length of 32 inches and a weight of just over 9lb. It had the unique 33-round detachable box magazine loading from the top and had a cyclic rate of fire of 700 rounds per minute. Its range was limited to 230 feet. (*AWM*)

(**Above**) The crew of an Australian 'short' 25-pounder artillery piece is pushed into position in its weapon pit in the Doiabi River area in the Central Sector in late November 1944, to cover the eastward movements of the 9th Infantry Battalion to capture Little George and Artillery Hills. Ultimately, the battalion's target of Pearl Ridge would also be seized with artillery support from guns, such as this one dubbed 'Snifter'. These 'short' 25-pounders had been parachuted or air-transported into New Guinea and used successfully, although some gunners believed that they were less accurate than the standard 25-pounder field artillery piece. As shown, there is no gun-shield for the crew, which exposed them to the possibility of a muzzle-blast and ensuing harm. (*AWM*)

(**Above**) A Matilda Infantry ('I') Tank from the 2/4th Armoured Regiment crosses the Sindou Creek at a 'corduroy road' ford along the Buin Road in order to support the 24th Infantry Battalion, the latter of which had its tractor train ambushed by the Japanese in the Southern Sector offensive on 26 April 1945. This was the initial use of Australian tanks in the Southern Sector offensive. These Matildas were long obsolete by European and North African standards of combat. The jungle terrain also limited all tanks, especially these heavier ones, in cross-country movement that restricted them to jungle tracks and rudimentary roads. However, the Matildas were quite adept at reducing enemy bunkers with their 2-pounder gun firing solid shot or flame with the Matilda Mk IV 'Frog' variant. (*AWM*)

(**Opposite above**) Lieutenant General Masatane Kanda, previously the Japanese 6th Division commanding officer (*seated left*), and Vice Admiral Baron Tomeshige Samejima, commander of the 8th Japanese Fleet (*seated right*), sign the document of surrender of the Bougainville area enemy forces in front of Australian 2nd Corps Commanding General, Lieutenant General Stanley S. Savige (*seated background middle*), on 8 September 1945. (*AWM*)

(**Opposite below**) Two armed Australian sentries, the left one with his slung Short Magazine Lee-Enfield (SMLE) rifle and the right one holding his Owen Carbine gun, guard seated Japanese prisoners from Nauro Island, while others march in a loose formation into the internment camp in front of the watchtower on 19 September 1945. Note, their uniforms, boots and belts were not ragged and their general appearance was not emaciated. These were probably not front line troops and, most likely, they subsisted on crops they had cultivated in large gardens since their lines of communication with distant Japanese supply bases had been severed long before. (*AWM*)

Epilogue

The South Pacific and Solomon Islands campaign was always known as Halsey's 'Shoestring Theater'. The main US Navy drive was going to be across the Central Pacific under Admirals Nimitz and Spruance. Guadalcanal, in the Southern Solomons, had been seized to stop the Japanese south-eastern expansion, which was intended to sever the Allies' lines of communication from the United States to Australia and New Zealand. The New Georgia group of islands in the Central Solomons had been occupied by the Americans in order to secure bases at Munda and Vila for Allied air power to begin launching the aerial bombardment and neutral-ization of Rabaul during Operation *Cartwheel*. In addition, the Central Solomons campaign inflicted tremendous losses on all of the Japanese services, both in the island fighting and by drowning in attempts to reinforce the forward combat areas from rear echelon bases in comparison to those suffered by the Allies.

With Operation *Cartwheel* devised to encircle the Japanese bastion at Rabaul rather than invade it, the rationale for Halsey's South Pacific Force to invade Bougain-ville was to build more proximate fighter and bomber airfields than the Central Solomons offered. Halsey's choice for landing at Cape Torokina in Empress Augusta Bay allowed him to gain a beachhead in a relatively undefended part of Bougainville and to build his airfields. His amphibious forces would not have to repeat the struggle on New Georgia by fighting a numerous and entrenched enemy on the northern or southern parts of Bougainville near Buka and Buin respectively.

Halsey's calculations paid off handsomely as Japanese generals Imamura and Hyakutake of the 8th Area and 17th Armies respectively failed to utilize their large Bougainville garrisons to drive the American landing back into Empress Augusta Bay. They had always contended that Cape Torokina was a feint and the real invasion would be on the eastern side of Bougainville, at Kieta where the Japanese landed in 1942. Instead, after the 1 November 1943 landings at Cape Torokina, the Japanese did very little to combat the invasion, squandering several weeks while the Allies landed supplies and reinforcements and had their engineers construct the requisite fighter strip and bomber fields. Throughout the fighting in the Solomon Islands, the Japanese consistently underestimated the numbers of the Allied Forces and, once combat occurred, a rigid mindset developed preventing more elastic tactics to be employed.

The South Pacific campaign was an infantry and artillery war with concentration of manpower a requisite to victory. This was largely due to the unquantifiable dimension of terrain. In the Solomon Islands, thick jungle made air-strikes of only limited value while the foot soldier, supported by a heavy preponderance of artillery and armour, would make the necessary gains to achieve the objective defended by an extremely stubborn foe that would entrench and fight to the last. The war in the South Pacific did not achieve the headline status of Tarawa, the Marshalls, the liberation of the Philippines and Marianas, Iwo Jima and Okinawa, to name some of the more notable island battlefields. However, the fighting in the Solomons had drawn into it so much of the Japanese land, sea and air forces and *matériel* that it had become impossible for the Japanese High Command to repeatedly marshal their forces to make strong counter-attacks elsewhere. Most importantly, the war in the South Pacific had rendered Rabaul ineffective, from which the Japanese could either counter-attack from or stridently delay the Allied forces laying siege to it. Ultimately, the Allies would be able to move northwards from the South Pacific towards the Japanese Home Islands.

References

Bergerud, Eric. *Touched with Fire: The Land War in the South Pacific*. Penguin Books. New York, 1996.

Diamond, Jon. *New Guinea: The Allied Jungle Campaign in World War II*. Stackpole Books. Mechanicsburg, 2015.

Diamond, Jon. *Guadalcanal: The American Campaign against Japan in World War II*. Stackpole Books. Mechanicsburg, 2016.

Gailey, Harry A. *Bougainville 1943–1945: The Forgotten Campaign*. University of Kentucky Press. Lexington, 1991.

Gamble, Bruce. *Target: Rabaul: The Allied Siege of Japan's Most Infamous Stronghold, March 1943–1945*. Zenith Press. Minneapolis, 2013.

Hammel, Eric. *Munda Trail*. Avon Books. New York, 1989.

Horton, D.C. *New Georgia: Pattern for Victory*. Ballentine Books. New York, 1971.

Hoyt, Edwin P. *The Glory of the Solomons*. Stein and Day. New York, 1983.

James, Karl. *The Hard Slog: Australians in the Bougainville Campaign, 1944–45*. Cambridge University Press. Cambridge, 2012.

Johnston, Mark. *The Australian Army in World War II*. Osprey Publishing. Oxford, 2007.

Lord, Walter. *Lonely Vigil: Coastwatchers of the Solomons*. Viking Press. New York, 1977.

McGee, William L. *The Solomons Campaigns 1942–1943: From Guadalcanal to Bougainville. Pacific War Turning Point*. BMC Publications. Santa Barbara, 2010.

Miller, John, Jr. *Cartwheel: The Reduction of Rabaul*. Center of Military History, United States Army. Washington, D.C., 1990.

Rottman, Gordon L. *Japanese Army in World War II: The South Pacific and New Guinea, 1942–43*. Osprey Publishing. Oxford, 2005.

Stille, Mark. *Guadalcanal 1942–43. America's First Victory on the Road to Tokyo*. Osprey Publishing. Oxford, 2015.

Toll, Ian W. *The Conquering Tide: The War in the Pacific Islands, 1942–1944*. Norton. New York, 2015.

Yenne, Bill. *The Imperial Japanese Army. The Invincible Years 1941–42*. Osprey Publishing. Oxford, 2014.